Avenues

Practice Book

HAMPTON-BROWN

Contents

Unit 1 | Family Album

Grandma's Records

We Honor Our Ancestors

Unit 2 | Earth: The Inside Story

Piecing Earth and Sky Together

Planet Earth/Inside Out

Unit 3 | Bodies in Motion

Dancing Wheels

Moving

Unit 4 | Freedom's Trail

Joining the Boston Tea Party

George Washington

Unit 5 | From Sea to Shining Sea

Greetings from America

The Bunyans

Unit 6 | It's Electrifying!

Ben Franklin's Experiment

Switch On, Switch Off

Unit 7 | Going Places with Patricia McKissack

Goin' Someplace Special

Getting to Someplace Special

Unit 8 | We the People

Calling the Doves

Coming to America

Name ______________________ Date ______________

Vocabulary: Key Words

The World of Music

Work with a partner. Add to this word web.

Write words about music.

Key Words
album
band
capture
pack
play
record

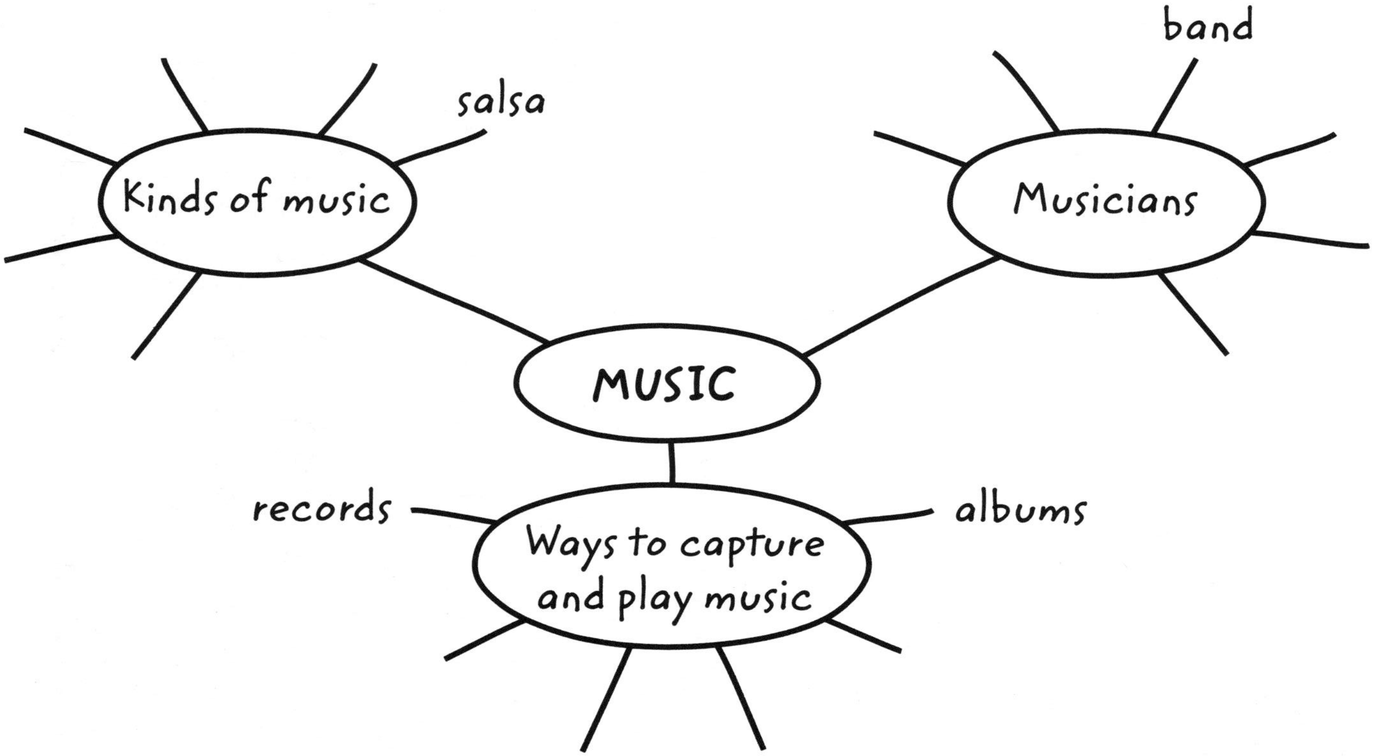

Name ______________________________ Date ______________

Grammar: Subject and Predicate

Parts of a Sentence

Study the examples in the box.

Write *S* for each statement below. Write *C* for each command.

In each statement, draw one line under the subject and two lines under the predicate.

Sentences

A sentence has two main parts. The **subject** tells whom or what the sentence is about. The **predicate** tells what the subject is, does, or has.

- A **statement** tells something.

  The boy chooses records.

  subject **predicate**

- A **command** tells someone to do something. The subject is not named, but it is always "you."

  Choose a record.

S 1. Ana dances to salsa music all the time.

____ 2. My grandmother has many records.

____ 3. This song is her favorite.

____ 4. She sings it in Spanish.

____ 5. Play that song again.

____ 6. No, put on this record.

____ 7. That music sounds very nice.

____ 8. Dance with me!

____ 9. This band comes to our town next week.

____ 10. Tell all your friends!

MORE Subjects and Predicates

Say a subject. Have a partner add a predicate to finish the sentence.

Name ______________________________ Date ______________

Vocabulary Skill

Multiple-Meaning Words

Read the meanings for each word. Then read the sentences.

Draw a line from each meaning to the sentence that uses the same meaning.

Underline the words that help you know which meaning is correct.

address

1. To speak to a group of people	Jaime is new here. His **address** is 914 Elm Street.
2. Information that tells where a building is located	Our teacher will **address** the new students tomorrow.

country

3. A nation, such as the United States	Jaime just moved from Mexico to this **country**.
4. Land where there are farms but no cities	His family lived on a farm in the **country**.

ring

5. To make the sound of a bell	When we heard the bell **ring**, we all got up to meet Jaime.
6. A circle	We stood in a **ring** around him.

letter

7. A written message sent by mail or e-mail	I spelled *Jaime* with the wrong **letter**. I used *H* instead of *J*.
8. A symbol that stands for a sound in the alphabet	I wrote a **letter** to my friend. I told her about Jaime.

Name ______________________ Date ____________

Grammar: Simple Subject

Keep It Simple!

Read each sentence.

Underline the complete subject. Then circle the simple subject.

Simple Subjects

The **complete subject** includes all the words that tell about *who* or *what*.

The **simple subject** is the most important **noun** in the subject.

1. My big sister loves music.
2. Students in her class sing with her.
3. A singer in our town teaches her.
4. My younger brother also sings all the time.
5. Our old dog always barks at him.
6. The whole family plays music after dinner.
7. My friends at school like my voice, too.
8. Many people sing in our family.

MORE Simple Subjects

Work with two partners. One person names a simple subject. The next person uses it to make a complete subject. The third person adds a predicate to make a complete sentence.

Name ______________________ Date ____________

Graphic Organizer: Story Map

Grandma's Records

Review "Grandma's Records."

Complete the story map.

Characters

Boy (the grandson)
Grandma
Grandma's nephew, Sammy

Setting

Beginning

The boy visits his grandmother for the summer. They dance and listen to music.

Middle

1. Sammy and his friends visit Grandma.
2. Sammy gives Grandma concert tickets.
3.
4.
5.

End

Name ________________________________ Date ______________

Comprehension Skill

Draw Conclusions

Read the passage below. Think about how to draw conclusions.

Gifts from Hungary

1 On my mother's birthday, a package arrived from my grandparents. They live in Hungary. That's a country in Europe.

2 There were three gifts in the box. Each gift was wrapped with colorful paper and ribbons. We hurried to open them.

3 One gift was a white tablecloth. It had red and orange flowers around the edges. Another gift was a huge box of chocolate candy.

4 The third gift was a book. My mother started to cry when she saw it. "It's my father's sketchbook!" she smiled.

5 "I didn't know Grandpa was an artist," I said. I have a sketchbook, too. I draw all the time. I wanted to see Grandpa's drawings.

6 We all gathered around. Mom put the book on her lap and opened it slowly. The pages were filled with wonderful drawings.

7 My father leaned over and cried, "Oh, Eva, that's you!" Eva is my mother's name. We all looked at the drawing of a little girl dancing. She wore a long dress. The dress had flowers on it, like the flowers on our new tablecloth.

8 "That's not Mom. It's a little girl!" my brother shouted. Everyone laughed.

9 "That is your mother," said my father. "She was a beautiful little girl, and she is beautiful now," he said softly. I was very proud of my grandfather. He is a fine artist.

Now take the test on page 11.

Name ______________________________ Date ______________

Test Strategy
Read parts of the story again.
Then choose your answer.

Read each item. Choose the best answer.

1 Which detail helps you draw the conclusion that the family was excited about the gifts?

- ⬭ There were three gifts.
- ⬭ They hurried to open the gifts.
- ⬭ They got a package from Hungary.
- ⬭ The narrator says that she draws all the time.

2 Look at the diagram.

Detail:		**Detail:**		**Conclusion:**
The grandfather sent his sketchbook to his family in the United States.	+	The mother cried and smiled when she saw the sketchbook.	=	

What is the best conclusion you can draw?

- ⬭ She is sad to see the sketchbook.
- ⬭ She does not feel well on her birthday.
- ⬭ She is happy that her father sent the sketchbook.
- ⬭ She is sorry that she did not send her parents a gift.

3 At the end of the story, what conclusion can you draw about the narrator?

- ⬭ She likes the candy more than the drawings.
- ⬭ She thinks her grandfather's drawings are very good.
- ⬭ She thinks her grandfather's drawings are not very good.
- ⬭ She thinks her drawings are better than her grandfather's.

Name ______________________ Date ____________

Research Skill

Use a Dictionary

live ➤ long

live[1] To be alive or have life.
live (liv) *verb.*

live[2] That is done in person, in front of an audience.
live (līv) *adjective.*

lizard A small reptile similar to a snake but with four legs.
liz•ard (liz′ərd) *noun.*

load 1. Something that is carried. *Noun.* 2. To put in or on: *Load the groceries in the car. Verb.*
load (lōd) *noun; verb.*

lobster A sea animal with large claws.
lob•ster (lob′stər) *noun.*

Study the part of a dictionary page shown above.

Write the answer to each question.

1. What part of speech is ***lobster***? "Lobster" is a noun.
2. What is the first guide word? ______________________
3. Could the entry word ***laundry*** appear on this page? Explain your answer.
____
4. Your mom says, "Carry the ***load*** up the hill." In her sentence, is ***load*** a noun or a verb? ______________________
5. If you could see the rest of the page, what would be the last entry word?
____

MORE Practice with the Dictionary

Work with a partner. Look up the word ***place*** in the dictionary.

Say a sentence that uses ***place*** as a noun. Have your partner say one that uses it as a verb.

Name ______________________________ Date ______________

Vocabulary: Key Words

Family Words

Write a Key Word to complete each sentence.

Key Words
adventure
ancestor
comfort
courage
heritage
presence
proud
trust

1. My great-grandmother Lalita is one of my ancestors.
2. She was brave. She had a lot of ______________ to travel here alone from India.
3. Her trip to America was exciting! It was a great ______________.
4. She taught her children about the songs and foods from India.

   They were part of her ______________.
5. I feel her ______________ whenever my father talks about her.
6. We are all ______________ that she is our ancestor.
7. My parents always ______________ me and make me feel better when I have a problem.
8. I ______________ them because I know they really care about me.

MORE Key Words Practice

Interview some family members. Ask about your family history. Then use some of the Key Words to write a paragraph about your ancestors.

Name ______________________ Date ____________

Grammar: Simple Predicate

I Write About My Family

Read each sentence.

Underline the complete predicate. Then circle the simple predicate.

> **Simple Predicate**
>
> The **complete predicate** tells what the subject **is** or **does**.
>
> The **simple predicate** is the **verb**, the most important word in the predicate.

1. My grandpa writes poems.
2. I like his poems a lot.
3. Grandma creates stories for children.
4. She tells the stories to our family.
5. My friends read Grandma's books.
6. My uncle works for a newspaper.
7. He is a reporter.
8. His articles give information about sports.
9. Everyone in my family writes something!
10. I am a writer, too.

MORE Simple Predicates

Work with two partners. One person names a subject. The next person adds a simple predicate (a verb). The third person adds more to the predicate to make a longer sentence.

Name ______________________________ Date ______________

Vocabulary Skill

Suffixes

Study the suffix chart.

Then read each sentence.

Write a word with a suffix that means the same as the words under the blank.

Suffix Chart

Suffix	Meaning
-able	can be/can give
-y	like
-en	made of
-ful	full of
-er	a person who

1. My grandmother gave me a ___beautiful___ (full of beauty) present for my birthday.

2. It is a green ____________ (made of wool) hat.

3. It feels soft and ____________ (like silk).

4. I am very ____________ (full of care) to keep it clean.

5. It is ____________ (can be washed), but only in cold water.

6. My grandmother is also a great ____________ (person who bakes).

7. She made me a delicious birthday cake with ____________ (like cream) chocolate frosting.

8. I had a ____________ (full of wonder) party!

MORE Suffixes

Write a paragraph about a gift you received. Use at least three words that end with suffixes from the suffix chart.

Name ______________________________ Date ______________

Grammar: Subject-Verb Agreement

We Sing and Dance

Read each sentence.

Write the correct verb in each blank.

When to Add -s

- If an action verb tells what one other person or thing does, add **-s** at the end.

  The girl **sings**.

- Do not add **-s** to an action verb when the subject names more than one.

  The girls **sing**.

1. I ____dance____ to the music.
   dance / dances
2. My sister ______________ the guitar.
   play / plays
3. My brother ______________ while she plays.
   sing / sings
4. We all ______________ and have fun.
   laugh / laughs
5. My parents and grandparents ______________ us.
   join / joins
6. My grandmother ______________ us her favorite dance.
   show / shows
7. She ______________ it the "samba."
   call / calls
8. We ______________ while she dances.
   clap / claps

Name ______________________ Date __________

Grammar: Verbs *Has, Have*

Do You Have It?

Look at the picture.

Write *has* or *have* in each blank.

Rules for *Has* and *Have*

- Use ***has*** with ***he***, ***she***, and ***it***.
  She **has** black hair.
- Use ***have*** with ***I***, ***you***, ***we***, and ***they***.
  I **have** new shoes.

1. We ___have___ a lot of pets at our house.
2. I __________ a fish in a bowl.
3. My fish __________ big eyes.

4. My brother __________ two funny birds.
5. He __________ birds that talk.
6. They __________ loud voices!

7. Dad __________ a big dog.
8. The dog __________ floppy ears.
9. Do you __________ any animals at your house?

MORE *Has* and *Have*

Write one sentence with *have* and another with *has*. Draw a picture to go with each sentence.

Name ______________________________ Date ______________

Grammar: Verbs *Am, Is,* and *Are*

On the Team

Look at the picture.

Write *am, is,* or *are* in each blank.

Rules for *Am, Is* and *Are*

- Use ***am*** with ***I***.
  I **am** so happy!
- Use ***is*** with ***he***, ***she***, and ***it***.
  It **is** a happy day for us.
- Use ***are*** with ***you***, ***we***, and ***they***.
  We **are** the winners.

1. My father ____is____ a soccer coach.
2. He ______________ the coach of my brother Julio's team.
3. My cousins ______________ on the team, too.
4. They ______________ very good players.
5. Julio ______________ the captain of the team.
6. I ______________ here to watch him play.
7. We ______________ not on the same team, but I cheer for him!
8. ______________ you the new player on the team?
9. You ______________ lucky.
10. It ______________ one of the best teams in town!

Name ______________________ Date ____________

Graphic Organizer: Category Chart

We Honor Our Ancestors

Review "We Honor Our Ancestors."

Complete the chart.

Artist	Ancestors	How the Artist Feels and Why
Carl Angel	mother and father	He loves his parents. Their stories make him feel good and give him ideas for his paintings.
Hung Liu		
JoeSam.		
Patssi Valdez		

Name ______________________ Date ____________

Grammar: Subject-Verb Agreement

My Uncle Writes Stories

Read each sentence.

Write a verb in each blank.

Rules for Subjects and Verbs

For action verbs:

- Add ***-s*** to the verb if the subject is ***he***, ***she***, or ***it***.
- Do not add ***-s*** to the verb if the subject is ***I***, ***you***, ***we***, or ***they***.

For the verb *be*:

- Use ***am*** if the subject is ***I***.
- Use ***is*** if the subject is ***he***, ***she***, or ***it***.
- Use ***are*** if the subject is ***you***, ***we***, or ***they***.

1. My Uncle Louis ____writes____ stories about my family.
   write / writes
2. He ______________ us a new story every year when he visits.
   bring / brings
3. I ______________ a lot from his stories.
   learn / learns
4. They ______________ very funny.
   am / is / are
5. We all ______________ them together.
   read / reads
6. Grandfather ______________ always happy when he hears the stories.
   am / is / are
7. It ______________ great to have a writer in the family.
   am / is / are
8. I ______________ sure that someday I'll be a good writer, too.
   am / is / are

Name ______________________ Date ____________

Vocabulary Skill

Figurative Language: Similes

Complete each sentence with a simile. Use *like* or *as*.

> **Figurative Language**
>
> A **simile** uses ***like*** or ***as*** to compare two different things.
>
> He eats **like** a pig!

1. Your hair shines like gold.
2. My friend swims ______________________
3. That player is ______________________
4. My hands feel as dry ______________________
5. The hot sun is ______________________
6. Tara sings ______________________
7. This cookie is as hard ______________________
8. My brother can run ______________________
9. This room looks ______________________

Complete the first part of each of the following similes.

10. ______________________ as fast as a rabbit.
11. ______________________ as light as a snowflake.
12. ______________________ like a hungry bear.

Name ______________________ Date ____________

Vocabulary: Key Words

Words About Handiwork

Key Words
beauty
clever
contest
handiwork
material
stitching
superior
task

Circle the correct Key Word.
Then write the sentence.

1. It is not an easy ___task / clever___ to make a quilt.

   It is not an easy task to make a quilt.

2. Take some ___material / clever___ and sew it together.

   ____

3. Make sure your ___superior / handiwork___ is very good.

   ____

4. Be very careful with your ___stitching / superior___!

   ____

5. Use pretty colors and shapes to add ___beauty / task___ to your work.

   ____

6. With your ___clever / material___ hands, you can sew a wonderful quilt.

   ____

7. Your quilt will be ___handiwork / superior___ to other quilts.

   ____

8. You might win a ___task / contest___ with it!

   ____

Name ________________________________ Date ______________

Grammar: Plural Nouns (*-s*, *-es*)

All the Beautiful Things

Look at the picture. Read the paragraph.

Write the correct plural form of the noun in each blank.

Rules for Plurals

- To make most nouns plural, add **-*s***.

  river → river<u>**s**</u>

- If a noun ends in ***s***, ***ss***, ***ch***, ***sh***, ***x***, or ***z***, add **-*es***.

  branch → branch<u>**es**</u>

After Toh made the earth, she showed Koh the land, the ___plants___ (plant), and the __________ (animal). Koh saw tall __________ (mountain), __________ (bush) with __________ (flower) on them, and trees full of __________ (peach). There were two __________ (fox) watching some __________ (duck) swim in a clear stream. It was one of the most beautiful __________ (place) Koh had seen!

MORE Plural Nouns

Draw your own picture of the earth. Include any plants and animals you like. Use plural nouns to label them. Show your work to a partner.

Name ______________________ Date ____________

Grammar: Questions with *Do, Does, Is, Are*

The Make-a-Question Game

How to Play

The Make-a-Question Game

1. Play with a partner.
2. Spin the spinner for a question word.
3. Make up a question about "Piecing Earth and Sky Together."

   Does Toh make the earth?

4. Write your question on another sheet of paper. Be sure you begin with a capital letter and end with a question mark.
5. Read your question to your partner. Have your partner answer.
6. Take turns. Write as many questions as you can in 15 minutes.

Make a Spinner

1. Get a brad and a large paper clip.
2. Push the brad through the center of the circle.

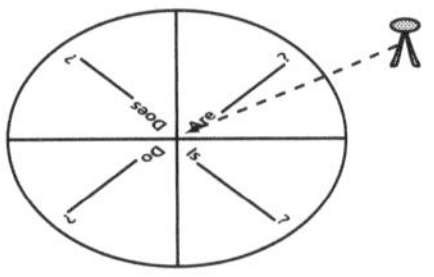

3. Open the brad.

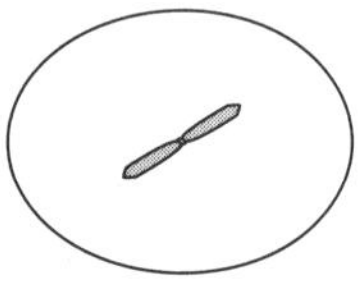

4. Hook the paper clip over the brad to make a spinner.

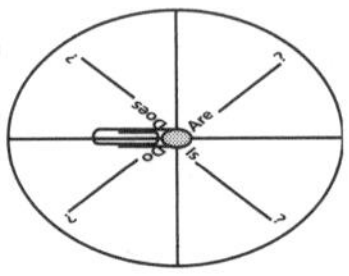

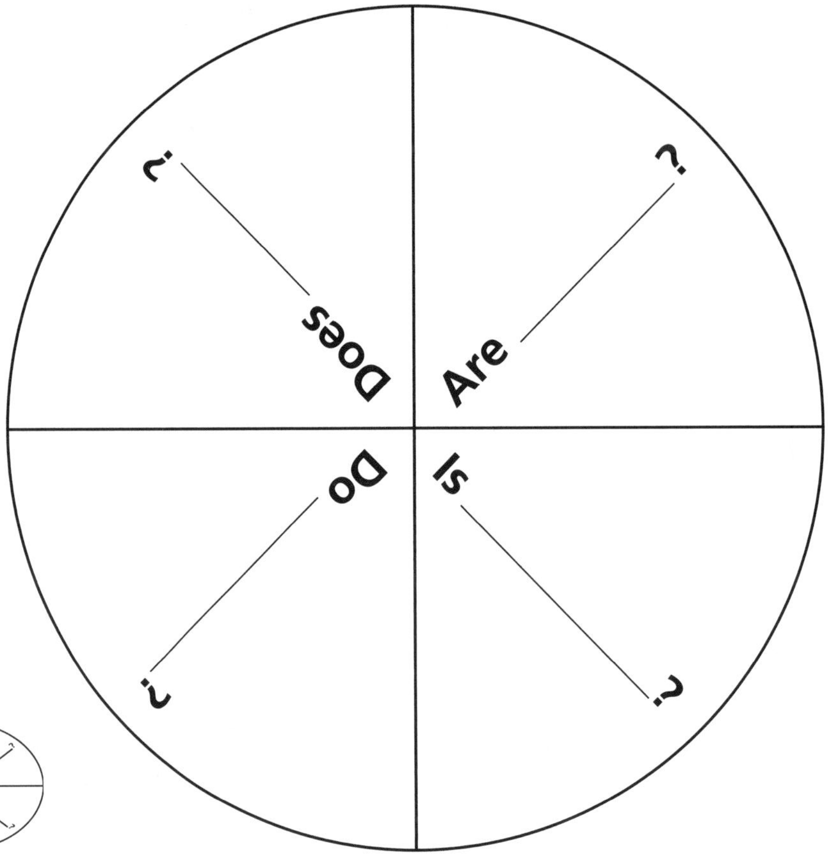

Name ______________________ Date __________

Grammar: Questions with *Wh-* Words

What Did You Do?

Review "Piecing Earth and Sky Together."

Write questions that you would like to ask Toh.

More Information, Please

When you want more information than just "yes" or "no," you can ask a question with one of these words:

who | ***what*** | ***where*** | ***when*** | ***why*** | ***which***

Make sure that you begin your question with a capital letter, and end it with a question mark.

1. What *are you going to sew next?*
2. Which ______________________
3. Why ______________________
4. Who ______________________
5. What ______________________
6. Where ______________________
7. When ______________________

MORE Questions and Answers

Show your questions to a partner.

Have your partner check your questions for correct capitalization and punctuation.

Then have your partner answer the questions the way Toh might answer them.

Name ______________________________ Date ______________

Literary Analysis

Characters' Motives and Conflicts

Think of a story you know that has two characters who don't agree.

Complete the map to tell about the story.

Story Title: ______________________________

Character: ____________________

What he or she wants:

Character: ____________________

What he or she wants:

Conflict:

What happens?

Name ______________________ Date ____________

Grammar: Plural Nouns

The Make-It-Plural Game

How to Play The Make-It-Plural Game

1. Play with a partner.
2. Spin the spinner for a singular noun.

3. Change the noun to a plural noun.
4. Write four sentences using the plural noun.

Plural Rules

- To make most nouns plural, add ***-s***.
  rock → rock**s**
- If the noun ends in ***s***, ***ss***, ***ch***, ***sh***, ***x***, or ***z***, add ***-es***.
  inch → inch**es**
- For nouns that end in a vowel plus ***y***, just add ***-s***.
  valley → valley**s**
- For nouns that end in a consonant plus ***y***, change the ***y*** to ***i*** and add ***-es***.
  sky → sk**ies**
- Some nouns change in special ways.
  man → men

Make a Spinner

1. Get a brad and a large paper clip.
2. Push the brad through the center of the circle.

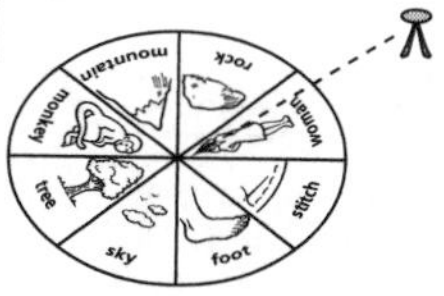

3. Open the brad.

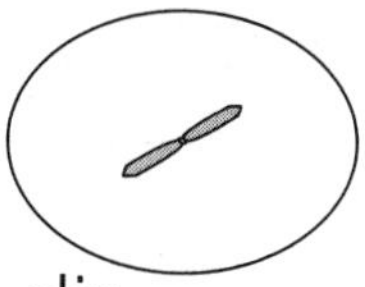

4. Hook the paper clip over the brad to make a spinner.

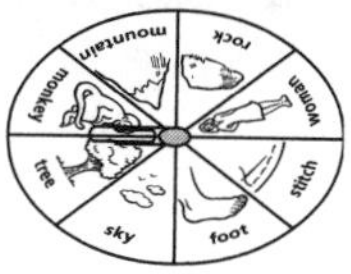

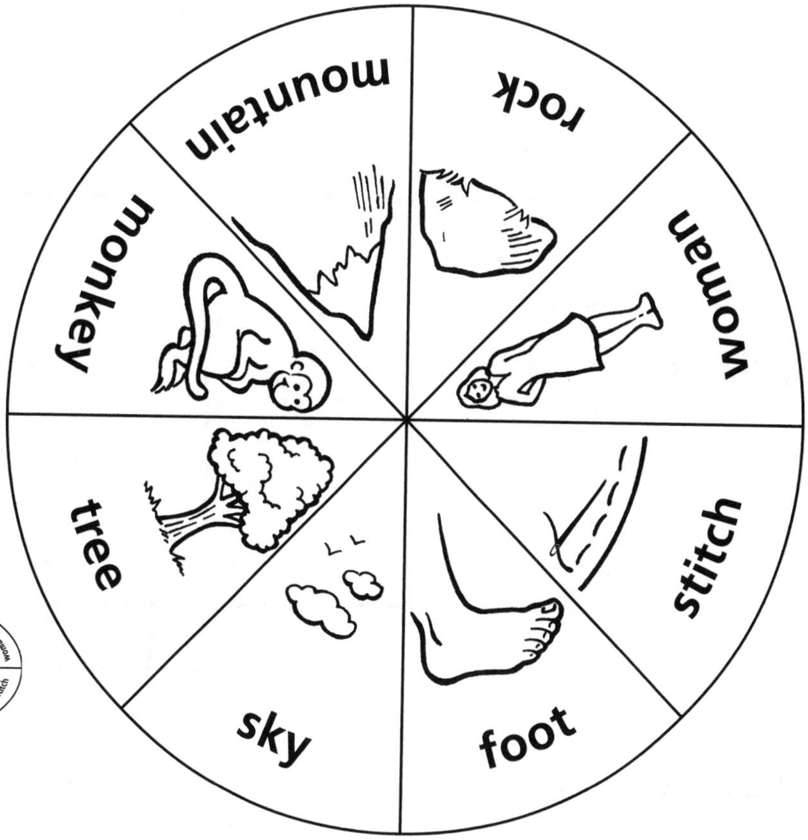

Name ______________________ Date ____________

Graphic Organizer: Goal-and-Outcome Map

Piecing Earth and Sky Together

Review "Piecing Earth and Sky Together."

Complete the story map.

Goal: Koh and Toh want to make the earth and sky.

Koh's Action: He makes the sky quickly and falls asleep.

Toh's Action:

Obstacle:

Koh's Action:

Toh's Action:

Outcome:

For use with TE pp. T86–T87

Name ______________________________ Date ______________

Respond to Literature

A Very Special Character

Think of a character from a folk tale you have read or heard. Or create your own character.

Write a description of the character.

Character's Name ______________________________

What special powers does the character have? ______________________________

____

____

____

What does the character do in the story? ______________________________

____

____

____

____

____

____

____

____

____

____

Name ______________________________ Date ______________

Comprehension Skill

Identify Main Idea and Details

Read the passage below. Think about the main idea and the details.

The Earth's Crust

1 The Earth's crust is its surface, or outer layer. We live on the Earth's crust. When we walk outside, we walk on the crust. We grow flowers and food on the crust, and we build our homes on it.

2 The Earth's crust is mostly made of rocks and soil. There are many different kinds of rocks.

3 Gravel is made up of a lot of tiny rocks and pebbles. Gravel is used to make concrete. The sidewalk outside my house is made of concrete. The floor in my basement is also made of concrete.

4 There are also different kinds of soil, or dirt, in the Earth's crust.

5 Clay is one kind of soil. It's sticky and thick when it is wet. It gets hard when it is baked at high temperatures. People make pots out of clay.

6 Humus is another type of soil. It helps plants grow. It is made from dead plants and animals. Humus is dark brown or black. My older sister uses it in her garden.

7 Sand is loose soil. It is created when rocks are worn down by weather and wind. The sand at the beach feels soft on my bare feet.

Now take the test on page 31.

Name ______________________________ Date ______________

Test Strategy
Try to answer the question without reading the answer choices. Then compare your answer to the choices.

Read each item. Choose the best answer.

1 What is the main idea of paragraph 6 on page 30?

- ⬭ Sand is loose soil.
- ⬭ Humus is a kind of soil.
- ⬭ Humus is the soil my mother uses.
- ⬭ Humus is not used for making sidewalks.

2 Which detail belongs in the box?

Main Idea—Article
The Earth's crust is made of rocks and different kinds of soil.

Detail:	**Detail:**	**Detail:**
Clay is a kind of soil that gets hard when it is baked.	Gravel is made of tiny rocks and pebbles.	

- ⬭ People make pots out of clay.
- ⬭ My basement floor has gravel in it.
- ⬭ My sister uses humus in her garden.
- ⬭ Humus is made from plants and animals.

Name ______________________________ Date ______________

Research Skill

Use a Dictionary

Study the dictionary entries on this page.
Then read the directions on page 33.

size ➤ sleek

size **1.** How large or small a thing is: *What is the size of your house?*
2. Amount or number: *I can't believe the size of your allowance! Noun.*
○ To arrange by size: *He sized the eggs and put the small ones in boxes. Verb.*
size (sīz) *noun; verb.*

skateboard A short board on wheels used for riding and to perform stunts.
skate•board (skāt´bord) *noun.*

skip **1.** To move by hopping on one foot and then the other. **2.** *(Informal)* To choose not to go to an event or activity: *I feel sick, so I'll skip the party.*
skip (skip) *verb.*

skunk A small, black animal with a bushy tail and white stripes on its back. It sprays a bad-smelling oil when it is scared.
skunk (skungk) *noun.*

sky The area you can see high above the ground, the trees, and the buildings: *The sky is blue today.*
sky (skī) *noun.*

WORD HISTORY

***Sky* comes from Middle English. It comes from an Old Norse word meaning "cloud."**

slam **1.** To close or shut with force and noise: *Don't slam the door!* **2.** To hit or throw with great force: *I heard Jim slam the book on the desk. Verb.*
○ The act or sound of slamming. *Noun.*
slam (slam) *verb; noun.*

sleek **1.** Smooth and shiny: *She brushed her hair until it was sleek.* **2.** Well-groomed and healthy looking. *Adjective.*
○ To make sleek or smooth: *The boy sleeks his horse after he rides it. Verb.*
sleek (slēk) *adjective; verb.*

Name ______________________________ Date ____________

Research Skill

Use a Dictionary

Study the dictionary page on page 32.

Write the answer to each question.

Dictionary Features

- A dictionary lists words in **alphabetical order**.
- The **definition** tells what the word means.
- The **pronunciation symbols** tell how to pronounce the word.
- The **part of speech** shows how the word can be used in a sentence.

1. What part of speech is ***skateboard***? noun
2. Does ***sky*** rhyme with ***pie***  or with ***key***?  ____________
3. Which word describes something smooth and shiny? ____________
4. What part of speech is ***skip***? ____________
5. Which word comes from an Old Norse word that means ***cloud***? ____________
6. What is the next entry in alphabetical order after ***skunk***? ____________
7. Which noun names an animal? ____________
8. What meaning of ***skip*** goes with the following sentence? *After I hurt my foot, I* ***skipped*** *to the sidelines.* ____________
9. Does ***slam*** rhyme with ***ham*** or with ***game***? ____________
10. What do people use skateboards for? ____________
11. Which word describes what you do when you close a door hard and make a loud noise? ____________
12. What is the first entry on the page? ____________

Name ______________________ Date ____________

Vocabulary: Key Words

Earth Words

Key Words
core
crust
earthquake
fault
gravity
mantle
plate
volcano

Look at the illustration.

Complete each sentence with a Key Word.

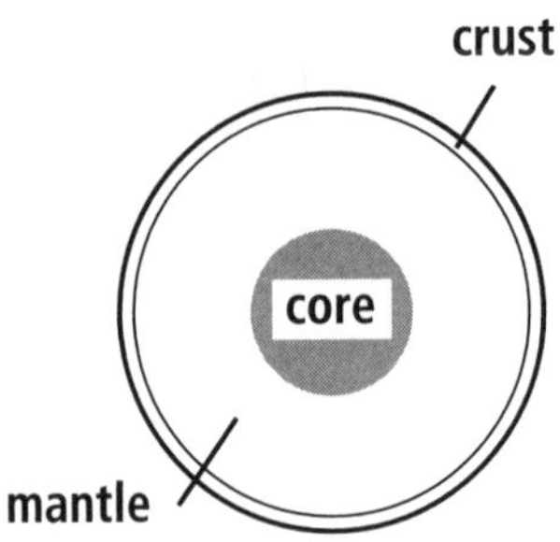

1. The ____crust____ is the outside layer, or part, of Earth.
2. The layer just under the crust is called the ______________.
3. The center of Earth is called the ______________.

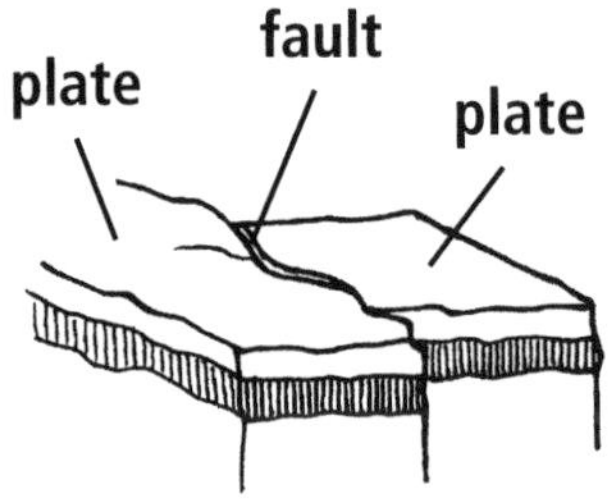

4. The crust is broken into large pieces called ______________.
5. A ______________ is a crack between plates in Earth's crust.
6. An ______________ happens when plates rub against each other.
7. Lava comes from the top of a ______________.
8. The force of ______________ pulls the lava down. It is the force that keeps things on the ground.

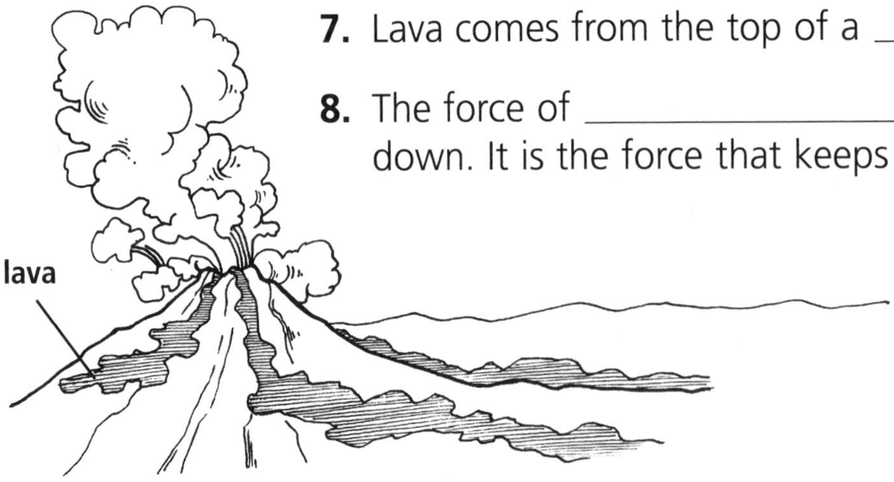

Name ______________________ Date ______________

Grammar: Count and Non-Count Nouns

You Can Count on It

Read each sentence. Look at the noun in dark type.

Write *COUNT* if you can count the noun. Write *NON-COUNT* if it is something you cannot count.

Count and Non-Count Nouns

You can **count** most nouns. They have a singular and a plural form.

Some nouns **cannot be counted**. They have only one form.

COUNT 1. Earth is a **planet** that moves around the sun.

______ 2. It has the **air**, sunlight, and water that plants and animals need.

______ 3. Earth has areas of **water** called oceans.

______ 4. It also has areas of land called **continents**.

______ 5. Earth has been damaged by **pollution**.

______ 6. Pollution is **trash**, dirty air, and other things that hurt Earth.

______ 7. There is a lot of **information** we can use to help us protect Earth.

______ 8. We must protect the air, water, and every **resource** on Earth.

MORE Count and Non-Count Nouns

Reread page 97 in your book.

Write all the count nouns on the page. Have a partner write all the non-count nouns.

Compare and discuss your lists.

Name ______________________ Date ____________

Grammar: Common and Proper Nouns

Particular People

Is It Common or Proper?

A **common noun** names any person.

A **proper noun** names a particular person.

Each important word in a proper noun is capitalized, including titles such as ***Dr.*** or ***Mrs.***

Read the paragraph. Find all the people nouns.

Write the people nouns in the correct column of the chart below.

My neighbors do different kinds of work. Mrs. Wong is a teacher. Rita Burke is a writer. Dr. Lewis is a dentist. Maria is a dancer. Mr. Franco is a baker. Aunt Helen is an artist. The boy next door wants to fly airplanes. His sister fixes cars. I think these jobs are great, but I want to be a scientist and study the Earth!

Common People Nouns	Proper People Nouns
neighbors	Mrs. Wong

Name ______________________________ Date ______________

Grammar: Common and Proper Nouns

Particular Places

- **Read the letter.**
- **Check for errors.**
- **Capitalize each proper noun.**

Place Names

A **common noun** names a **type** of place.

planet continent ocean

A **proper noun** names a **specific** place.

Earth North America Pacific Ocean

Each important word in a proper noun is capitalized.

Dear Gonzalo,

C

Last week we went on a trip to ~~c~~alifornia. First we went to lake Tahoe. It's up in the sierra nevada, a very impressive group of mountains. We snowboarded there at a place called sutter Peak. Then we drove over the Golden gate Bridge to visit my uncle in san francisco. Next we drove through the Central valley. We passed the sacramento River and saw many miles of farmland. Then we drove by the san Gabriel Mountains toward the city of Los angeles. There, we swam at the beach in santa monica.

I had fun in California. I'll tell you more about it when you come to visit.

Your friend,

Jeffrey

Name ______________________ Date ______________

Grammar: Possessive Nouns

Let's Get Possessive

Read the paragraph.

Change each group of underlined words to a phrase that uses a possessive noun.

Then rewrite the paragraph.

We now understand the origin of Earth better. There was a big cloud of dust in space. The particles that belonged to the cloud began to stick together. The size of the planet grew and grew. Then the surface of the young planet became hard and the temperature of the surface cooled. A large land mass formed. This was known as Pangaea. The land that belonged to Pangaea slowly split apart into smaller masses. Today, the environment of Earth is just right for plants and animals.

We now understand Earth's origin better.

____

____

____

____

____

____

Name ______________________________ Date ______________

Grammar: Common and Proper Nouns

Visit to a Volcano

Read the letter.

Capitalize the proper nouns.

> **Common and Proper Nouns**
>
> A **common noun** names any person, place, or thing.
>
> A **proper noun** names a particular person, place, or thing.
>
> Each important word of a proper noun is capitalized.

Dear Sara,

My whole class went on a trip to Mount Saint Helens. That is a volcano in the state of washington. On may 18, 1980, at 8:32 on a sunday morning, the magma and gas pushed up and out the top of the mountain. There was an earthquake. Rock and ice broke off the mountain and fell down into spirit Lake, and some of it went into the Toutle river. At the Johnston ridge Observatory, we saw the crater and the land all around. I hope you get to see it, too. It was a great day.

Your friend,

Benita

Name ______________________ Date ____________

Graphic Organizer: Main Idea Chart

Planet Earth/Inside Out

Review "Planet Earth/Inside Out."

Complete the main idea chart. The chart continues on page 41.

Section	Important Details	Main Idea
Earth's Formation	• Gases and dust pulled together 4.6 billion years ago. • The planet became hard on the outside. • Most of Earth became covered with water. • Pangaea began to split apart into continents 250 million years ago.	Scientists think Earth was formed over millions of years.
Earth's Layers		
A Planet in Motion		

Name ______________________ Date ____________

Graphic Organizer: Main Idea Chart

Planet Earth/Inside Out

Complete the main idea chart that you started on page 40.

Section	Important Details	Main Idea
Sudden Movements of the Earth		
Volcanic Eruptions		
Changes to Earth's Surface		

Name ______________________ Date ____________

Grammar: Plural Nouns

Volcanoes and Earthquakes

Rules for Plurals

Count nouns have a **singular** and a **plural** form.

- To make most nouns plural, add ***-s***.
  plate → plate**s**
- If the noun ends in ***s, ss, x, ch, sh,*** or ***z***, add ***-es***.
  stitch → stitch**es**
- For nouns that end in a consonant plus ***y***, change ***y*** to ***i*** and add ***-es***.
  sky → sk**ies**

Non-count nouns only have one form.

gravity lava
magma air

Study the rules.

Read the report.

Write the correct form of the noun to complete each sentence.

Two Natural Disasters

Volcanoes and earthquakes (earthquake) are caused by the Earth's shifting ______ (plate). As the plates crash against each other, ______ (mountain) are pushed up. The surface of the Earth is wrinkled, creating deep ______ (valley). An earthquake moves the ______ (ground). Some destroy ______ (building).

A volcano erupts when pressure pushes ______ (magma) and hot gases up from deep in the Earth. Ash fills the ______ (air), and ______ (stream) of lava flow down. Eruptions have destroyed several ______ (city) in the past.

Name ______________________ Date ____________

Comprehension Skill

Use Maps

Study the map.

Write the answer to each question.

How to Use a Map

- Read the title.
- Look at the labels.
- Study the legend and scale.

1. For which area does this map show information? California

2. Does the map show all the earthquakes in California? Explain your answer. ______________________

3. What country is south of California? ______________________

4. Which area shows more earthquakes—Los Angeles or Bakersfield? ______________________

5. What seems to be true about earthquakes and the San Andreas Fault? ______________________

6. How far is Bakersfield from Los Angeles? ______________________

7. Which city is farther from the San Andreas Fault—San Diego or Los Angeles? ______________________

Some Earthquakes in California 1800–2000

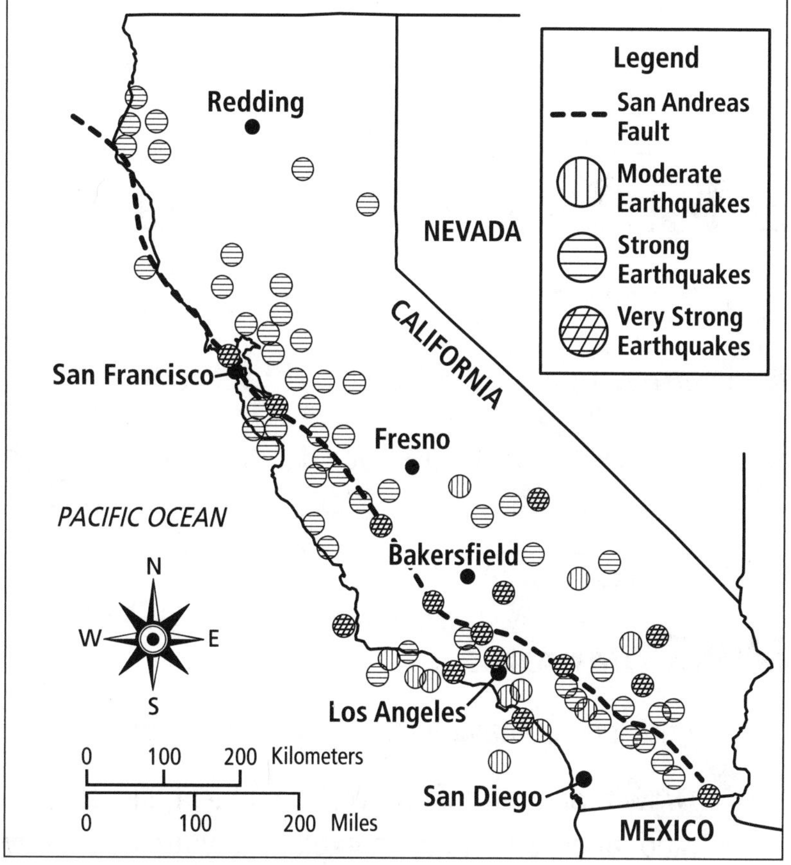

Name ______________________ Date ______________

Comprehension Skill

Use Diagrams

Study the diagram.

Write the answer to each question.

How New Crust Forms

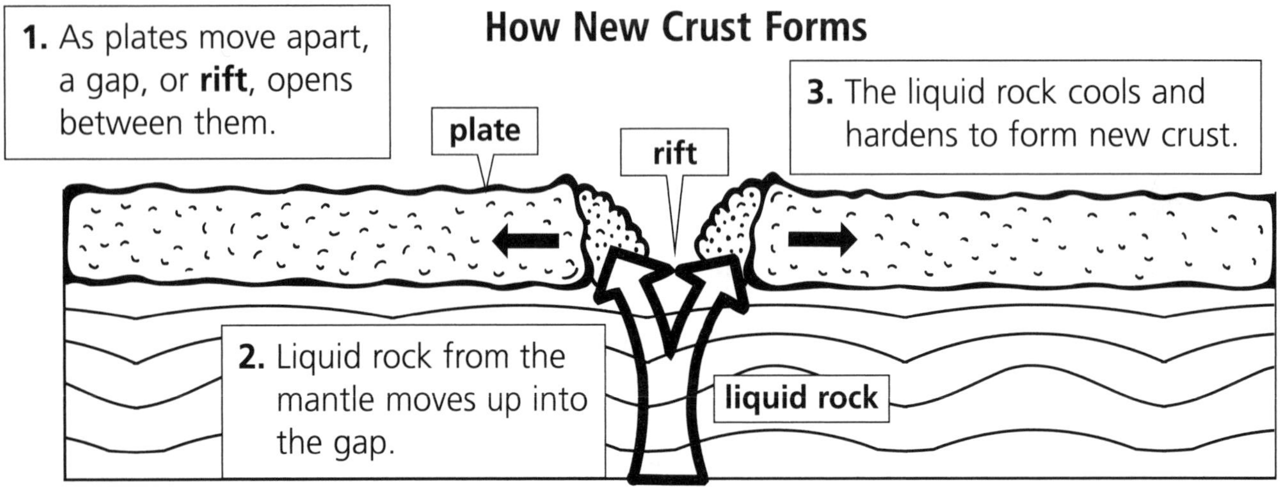

1. As plates move apart, a gap, or **rift**, opens between them.
plate
rift
3. The liquid rock cools and hardens to form new crust.
2. Liquid rock from the mantle moves up into the gap.
liquid rock

1. How is a gap between plates created?

____

2. What is a gap between plates called? ______________________

3. What fills a rift? ______________________________

4. From where does the liquid rock come? ______________________

5. How does the liquid rock turn into new crust?

____

MORE Diagrams

Imagine you have a visitor from outer space.

Draw a diagram of an everyday object, like a bicycle or a pen. Add labels and notes to explain to your visitor how it works.

Vocabulary: Key Words

Dancing Words

Key Words
audience
energy
expression
improve
movement
performance

Read each sentence.

Write *T* for true. Write *F* for false.

__T__ **1.** If people run very fast, they use a lot of **energy**.

_____ **2.** You **improve** something when you make it worse.

_____ **3.** An **audience** is the main dancer in a show.

_____ **4.** When you make a **movement**, you move parts of your body.

_____ **5.** When you see dancers in a show, you see a **performance**.

_____ **6.** If you have a lot of **energy**, you are tired all the time.

_____ **7.** Dancers show feelings when they use their bodies for **expression**.

_____ **8.** An **audience** claps and cheers if it likes a show.

MORE Key Words Practice

Tell your partner about a performance you have seen.

Try to use some of the Key Words to talk about it.

Name ______________________ Date ____________

Grammar: Subject Pronouns *I*, *We*, *You*

Would You Like to Dance?

Read each sentence.

Write *I*, *you*, or *we* to complete each sentence.

1.
Will ___you___ be my dance partner?
2.
Yes, __________ would like to be your partner.
3.
Have __________ ever taken dancing lessons before?
4.
No, __________ am here for my first lesson today.
5.
__________ will have fun dancing together!

Name ______________________ Date __________

Grammar: Negative Words

That Is Not True!

Negative Words

no not never no one nobody

Read each sentence.

Add a negative word or change a word to make a negative sentence.

Write the new sentence.

1. I am a good dancer.

   I am not a good dancer.

2. There are dancers in wheelchairs.

   ____

3. Everyone should do what he or she loves to do.

   ____

4. Dancing is boring.

   ____

5. Everybody should listen to the dance teacher.

   ____

6. It is always good to practice for a performance.

   ____

MORE Negative Words

Talk with a partner about each sentence. Which sentence of each pair do you agree with?

Share your opinions!

Name ______________________ Date ____________

Grammar: Subject Pronouns *He, She, It, They*

The Pronoun Game

How to Play The Pronoun Game

1. Play with a partner.

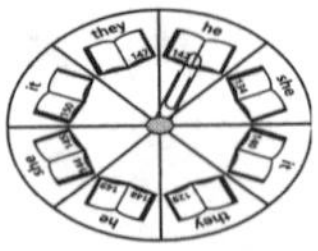

2. Spin the spinner.
3. Open "Dancing Wheels" to the page or pages on the spinner. Look at the picture. Find a noun (a person, place, or thing).
4. Make two sentences: one with the noun, and one with the pronoun on the spinner.

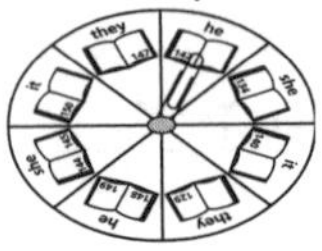

Devin dances.
He has fun.

5. Write your sentences on a sheet of paper.
6. Read your sentences to a partner.
7. Take turns.
8. See how many sentences you and your partner can write in fifteen minutes!

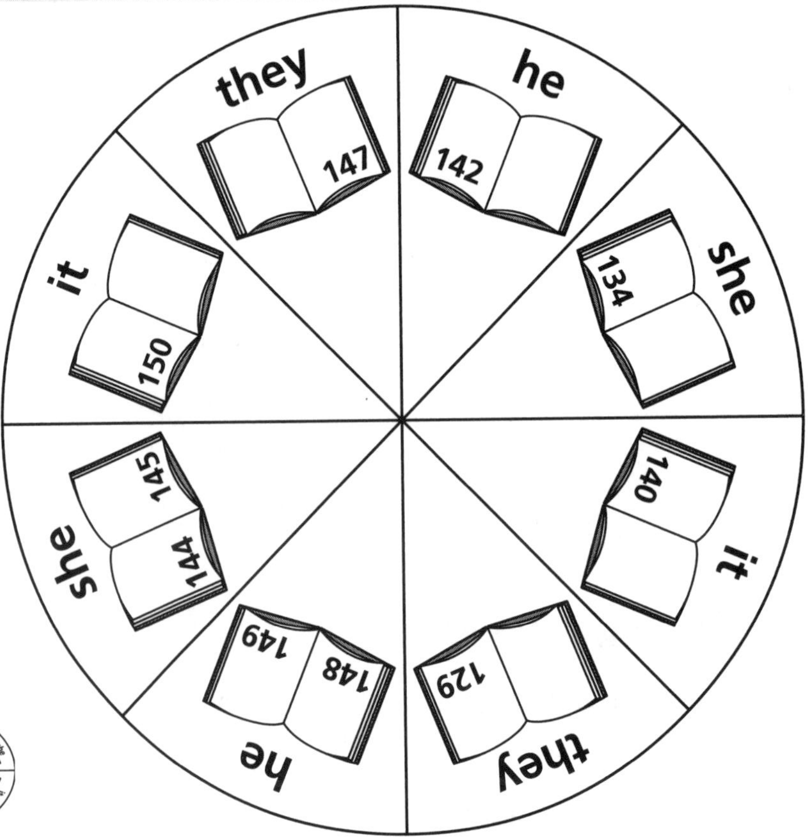

Make a Spinner

1. Get a brad and a large paper clip.
2. Push the brad through the center of the circle.

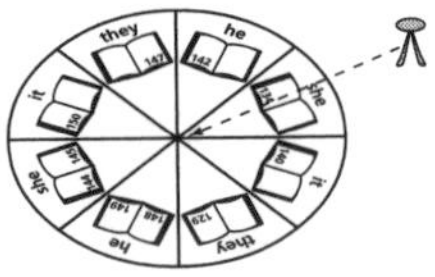

3. Open the brad.

4. Hook the paper clip over the brad to make a spinner.

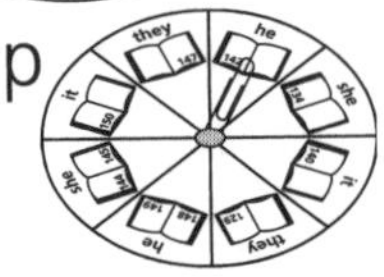

Name ______________________ Date __________

Grammar: Possessive Pronouns

Is Our Group Ready?

Read each sentence. Look at the underlined words.

Use a pronoun to rewrite the sentence.

Possessive Pronouns	
Some **pronouns** tell who owns or has something.	
One	**More than One**
my	our
your	your
his, her, its	their

1. Where are the dance shoes that you own?

   Where are your dance shoes?

2. They are in the bag that I own.

   ____

3. Is the partner that you have here?

   ____

4. Yes, Mia came with Mr. Blanco. She came in Mr. Blanco's car.

   ____

5. Are the costumes that you and Mia own clean?

   ____

6. Yes, the costumes that we own look great!

   ____

MORE Pronouns

Imagine that you and your partner are dancers.

Use pronouns to tell each other about your costumes.

Draw pictures of them.

Name ______________________ Date ____________

Grammar: Contractions

It's Possible!

Read pages 134–135 in "Dancing Wheels."

Read each sentence on this page.

Change the underlined words to a contraction.

Then rewrite the sentence.

Contractions

- Make contractions with ***am***, ***is***, and ***are*** like this:

I + am = I'm	he + is = he's
you + are = you're	she + is = she's
we + are = we're	it + is = it's

- Make contractions with ***not*** like this:

is + not = isn't	are + not = aren't

1. The doctors thought, "Mary is not going to live long."

   The doctors thought, "Mary isn't going to live long."

2. Her parents thought, "They are wrong."

   ____

3. Her parents decided, "We are not leaving her here."

   ____

4. They thought, "We are taking her home."

   ____

5. They told the doctors, "You are not keeping her here."

   ____

6. They told Mary, "It is possible for you to dance."

   ____

7. Mary decided, "I am a dancer."

   ____

Name ______________________ Date ____________

Graphic Organizer: Sequence Chain

Dancing Wheels

Review "Dancing Wheels."

Complete the sequence chain about Mary's life.

Mary Verdi-Fletcher

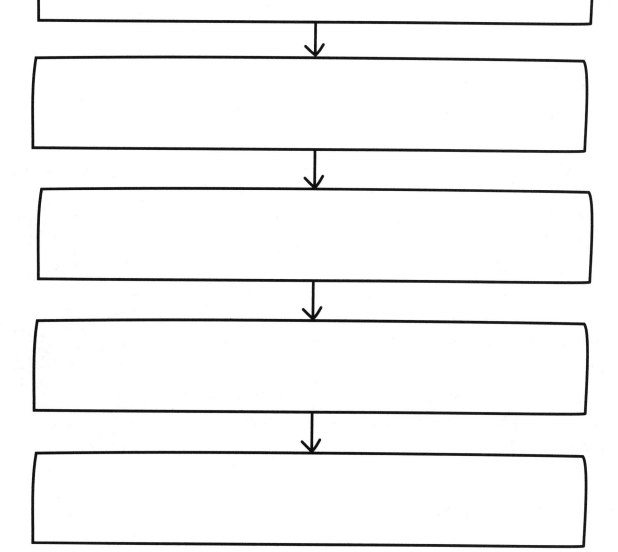

Mary was born with spina bifida in the 1950s.

↓

↓

↓

↓

Name ______________________ Date ____________

Vocabulary Strategy

Use Context Clues

Read the passage below. Think about how to use context clues.

The Teen Actors Group

1 Danny and Melinda put on their stage makeup. Jill and Marco put on their costumes. The Teen Actors Group is almost ready for their third performance. The group was started two years ago. Marco initiated the idea to form a group of teen actors. He brought everyone together. The seven members of the group are all from Chicago.

2 The Teen Actors Group performs for people who are in hospitals. Their goal is to help them recuperate. They want people to get better quickly. So far, they have performed for more than 40 people.

3 Marco says, "My sister was in the hospital three years ago. She was there for two weeks, and she didn't know what to do with herself all that time. That's how I got the idea to help people who are in the hospital for a long time."

4 Marco's friends thought he had a good idea. The people who work at the hospital loved the idea, too. Melinda says, "They were so happy that we wanted to perform for the people in need of care. Now they help us make our costumes and get everything ready for our shows."

5 Danny says, "We work very hard. We practice our roles over and over until we master them. That helps us give our best performance."

Now take the test on page 53.

Name ______________________ Date ____________

Test Strategy
Read all the answer choices before you choose your answer.

Read each item. Choose the best answer.

1 Read paragraph 1 on page 52. What does the word initiated mean?

- ⊂⊃ ended
- ⊂⊃ started
- ⊂⊃ hurried
- ⊂⊃ wasted

2 Read paragraph 2 on page 52. What does the word recuperate mean?

- ⊂⊃ to get sick
- ⊂⊃ to laugh
- ⊂⊃ to become strong and healthy again
- ⊂⊃ to perform in a play

3 Read the meanings of the word master.

master (**mas**-tur)

1. (verb) to understand well

2. (noun) a male teacher

3. (noun) a person who owns an animal

Which meaning best fits the way master is used in paragraph 5 on page 52?

- ⊂⊃ Meaning 1
- ⊂⊃ Meaning 2
- ⊂⊃ Meaning 3

Name ______________________________ Date ______________

Comprehension Skill

Facts and Opinions

Read Delia's letter to her grandmother.

Highlight each fact in one color. Highlight each opinion in another color.

Is That a Fact?

A **fact** is something that can be proved.

An **opinion** is an idea or belief about something.

Dear Grandma,

Last night I went to see a play in a theater. It was exciting to see all the actors on stage. The play was about a family. They came from Mexico to live in the United States. There was a grandmother in the play. She was a fun character. She told many stories about her life in Mexico. Her stories were very good, but I think yours are even better! We are coming to visit you soon. I think we will have lots of fun telling each other stories!

Love,

Delia

Name ______________________ Date ____________

Vocabulary: Key Words

Body Words

Key Words
bone
heart
joint
muscle
nerve
oxygen
skeleton
spinal cord

Think about how the parts of the human body work together.

Complete this word web. Use the Key Words and other words you know.

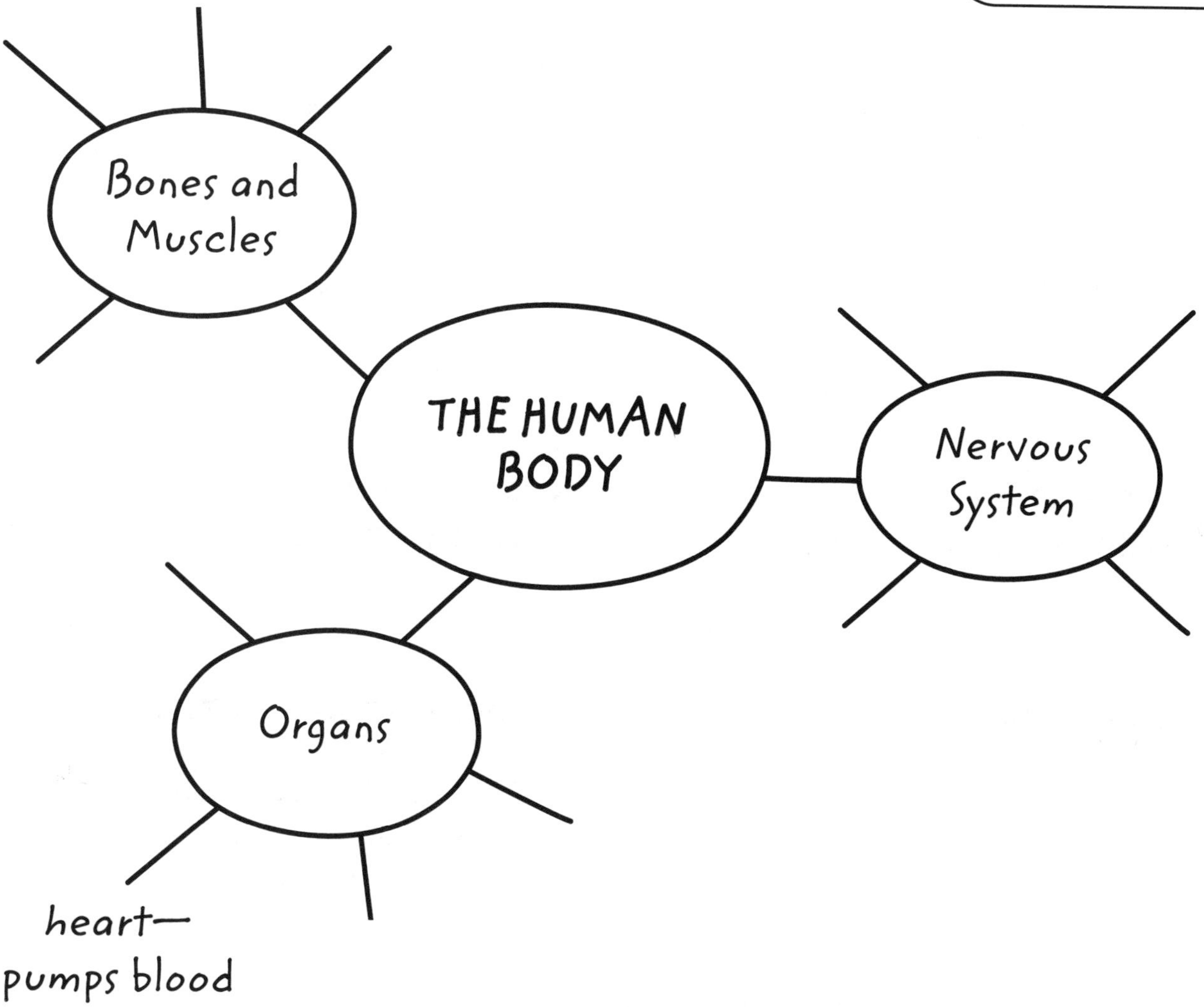

Name ______________________ Date __________

Vocabulary Skill

Use a Thesaurus

Work with a partner.

Read each entry word.

Write as many synonyms and antonyms as you can for each word.

Use a thesaurus to find more synonyms and antonyms.

Synonyms and Antonyms

Synonyms are words that are similar in meaning.

tiny small

Antonyms are words with opposite meanings.

go stop

happy, *adjective*
synonyms: glad, pleased, ______
______
antonyms: sad, unhappy, ______
______

pretty, *adjective*
synonyms: lovely, beautiful,
______
antonyms: ugly, unattractive,
______

warm, *adjective*
synonyms: hot, boiling, ______
______
antonyms: cool, chilly, ______
______

loud, *adjective*
synonyms: noisy, ______
______
antonyms: soft, quiet, ______
______

MORE Synonyms and Antonyms

Write four sentences. Describe a real or imaginary person. Then write four more sentences. Use antonyms to describe someone who is very different from the first person.

Name ______________________ Date ______________

Grammar: Prepositions

From Top to Bottom

Look at each picture. Read the sentence.

Write a prepositional phrase from the box to complete each sentence.

Prepositional Phrases

Prepositional phrases begin with short words called **prepositions**. Prepositional phrases help to tell more about something.

on your spine	with your muscles	of your body
for you		at the knee

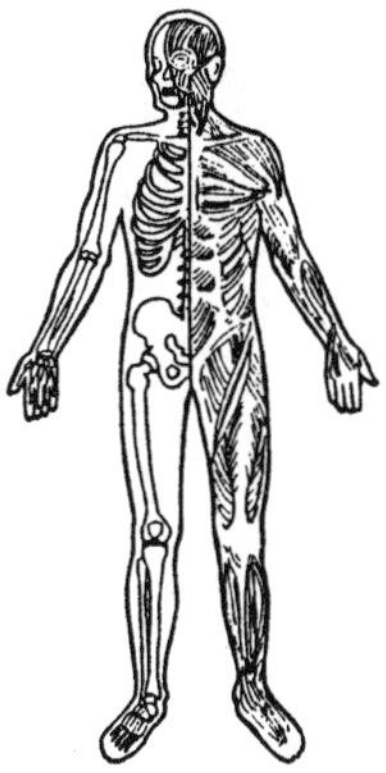

1. Your muscles and bones do a lot of things for you!

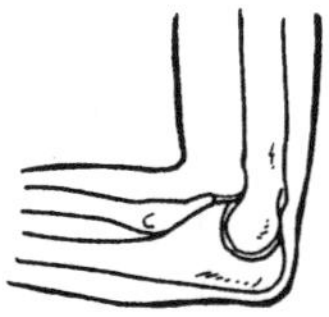

2. Joints are delicate parts ______________.

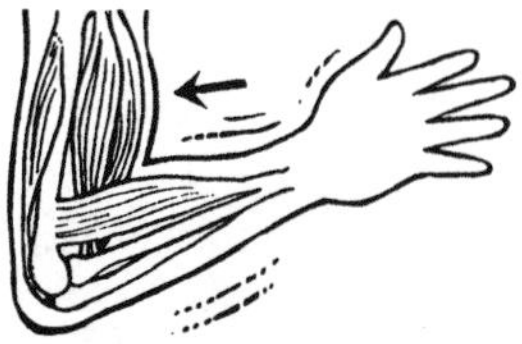

3. You move your arm ______________.

4. Your skull rests ______________.

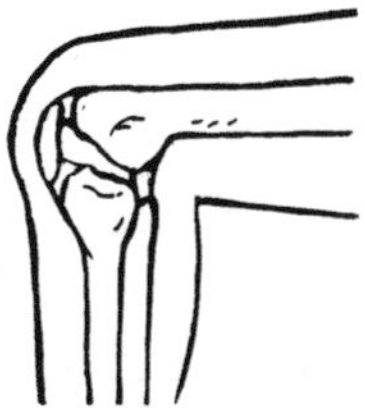

5. Your leg bends ______________.

Name ______________________ Date ____________

Grammar: Object Pronouns

Learn All About Them

Read the sentence. Look at the underlined words.

Change the underlined words to a pronoun. Then rewrite the sentence.

Object Pronouns

One	More than One
me	us
you	you
him, her, it	them

1. Can you bring that drawing of a skeleton to the teacher?

   Can you bring it to the teacher?

2. Sure, I'll give it to Mrs. Yang as soon as I find it.

   ____

3. I think Paco had it. Didn't you give it to Paco?

   ____

4. Yes, but Paco gave it to Lana and Kim yesterday.

   ____

5. She told Carlos and me that she wanted to check it.

   ____

6. Here it is! I'll copy it for Carlos and you.

   ____

MORE Object Pronouns

Work with two partners. Find a pen.

Take turns using object pronouns to give directions, such as *Give her the pen.* Have your partners follow your directions. Then follow your partners' directions.

Name ______________________ Date __________

Graphic Organizer: Word Map

Moving

Review "Moving."

Work with a group. Complete a word map for one part of the body: skeleton, joint, backbone, or muscle.

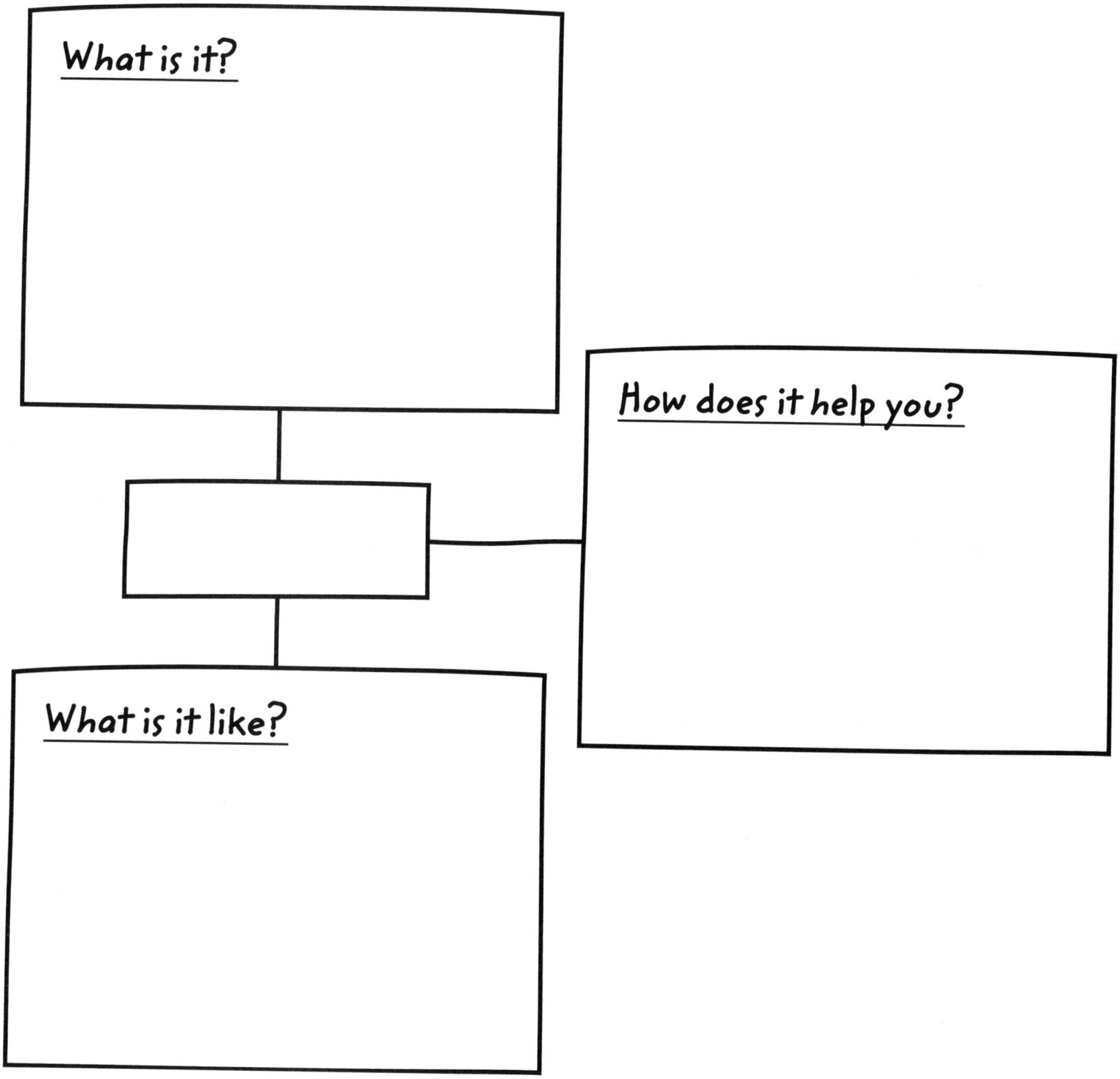

What is it?
How does it help you?
What is it like?

Name ______________________ Date __________

Grammar: Pronouns

Can You Meet Us There?

Read each sentence.

Circle the correct pronoun. Then write the sentence.

1. Will you play soccer with ___me / I___?
   Will you play soccer with me?
2. Can ___us / we___ play after school today?
3. Tommy, would you like to play with ___we / us___?
4. ___Me / I___ am the only one who has a ball!
5. Yes, we need your ball. Will you bring ___it / them___ to the field?
6. I'll bring it if you let Amy play. ___Her / She___ is a good player.
7. Then ask ___she / her___ to come!
8. If you know other players, bring ___they / them___ with you, too!

Name ______________________ Date __________

Vocabulary Skill

Use Suffixes

Read each sentence.

Write the correct word (noun or verb) to complete the sentence.

Suffixes

A **suffix** is a part added to the end of a word. It changes the word's meaning.

Verb	Suffix	Noun
move	-ment	movement
express	-sion	expression
protect	-tion	protection

1. This movement (move / movement) is hard to learn!

2. If you slip, this mat on the floor will give your body some ______________ (protect / protection).

3. The mat will ______________ (protect / protection) us when we practice, but there is no mat in the performance!

4. Can you ______________ (move / movement) over a little so I can see the teacher?

5. Our teacher says it is important to ______________ (move / movement) gracefully.

6. It is also important to dance with ______________ (express / expression).

7. That means that you ______________ (express / expression) feelings with your body.

MORE Suffixes

Work with a partner.

Read aloud each sentence. Explain how you figured out the pronunciation of each word with a suffix.

Name ______________________ Date ____________

Vocabulary: Key Words

Freedom Words

Read the paragraph.

Rewrite the paragraph on a separate sheet of paper. Replace the underlined words with the correct Key Word.

Key Words
colony
patriot
politics
representative
soldier
tax
traitor

The Road to Independence

Hundreds of years ago, people moved from Great Britain to America. They lived in thirteen settlements that belonged to Great Britain. The king of Great Britain needed money. So he asked the colonists to pay money to the government on the things they bought. The money went to Great Britain. Some people refused to pay. To King George III, anyone who did this was a person who hurt his country. To the colonists, however, this was a person who loved his country. The colonists wanted a person to speak for them in Great Britain. That person could tell King George III what was fair in the colonies. King George did not change his way of running the government. He sent persons in an army to the colonies. The colonists had to fight for their freedom.

Name ____________________ Date __________

Grammar: Regular Past Tense Verbs

A Trip to Boston

Complete the letter. Write the past tense form of each verb.

Rules for Past Tense Verbs

- Most verbs: push → push**ed**
- If it ends in a short vowel and a consonant: hop → ho**pp**ed
- If it ends in **e**: like → lik**ed**
- If it ends in a consonant and ***y***: try → tr**ied**

Dear Sonji,

I wanted (want) to tell you about my trip to Boston. I ________ (like) it a lot. We ________ (walk) the Freedom Trail. I ________ (learn) a lot about Paul Revere. He was a silversmith who ________ (create) beautiful trays and other things. He was also a patriot. He ________ (help) with the American Revolution. He ________ (hop) on his horse at midnight and ________ (complete) a long journey before dawn. He ________ (hurry) to warn the patriots that the British were coming. I'm glad I ________ (visit) Boston. I hope you get a chance to go there, too.

Sincerely,

Roberto

Name ______________________________ Date ______________

Grammar: Present and Past Tense Verbs

Who Is Samuel Adams?

Write the correct verb to complete each sentence.

Rules for *Is/Are, Was/Were*

	In the present	In the past
To tell about one person or thing	**is**	**was**
To tell about more than one	**are**	**were**

The man in the picture ___is___ (is / are) Samuel Adams. Sam Adams __________ (was / were) a hero in the American Revolution. His cousin __________ (was / were) John Adams, the second president of the United States. Sam Adams __________ (is / are) an interesting patriot to study. His speeches __________ (was / were) full of emotion. At that time, the colonists __________ (are / were) upset with the British. They believed the British tax on tea __________ (is / was) unfair. Many American colonists __________ (was / were) ready to fight. Sam Adams wrote letters that __________ (are / were) printed in the newspaper. Each letter __________ (is / was) a criticism of the British. Today, Americans __________ (is / are) proud of colonists like Sam Adams. Americans __________ (are / were) free today because the colonists fought for their beliefs.

Name ______________________ Date ______________

Graphic Organizer: Problem-and-Solution Chart

Joining the Boston Tea Party

Review "Joining the Boston Tea Party."

Complete the problem-and-solution chart.

Problems	Solutions
1. The colonists have to buy English goods, like cloth, at a high price.	They stop buying English goods.
2.	
3.	

Name ____________________ Date ____________

Comprehension Skill

Identify Fact and Opinion

Read the passage below. Look for facts and opinions.

A Man with a Plan

1 Samuel Adams was a leader of the American Revolution. He was born in Boston, Massachusetts. Some people believe that he is the most important person ever born in Massachusetts!

2 He was a representative in the government of Massachusetts. He knew almost everyone in Boston. Most people respected him and listened to his ideas.

3 One of his ideas was that it was not fair for England to tax the colonies. He wanted the colonists to be free. He wanted the colonies to keep their own tax money.

4 I think that Sam was very smart when he planned the Boston Tea Party. Many people believed that it was a good plan. They decided to help him.

5 Other people did not agree with Sam's ideas. They did not want to make the English rulers angry. They said that Sam wanted to break things and hurt people.

6 Sam did not want anyone to get hurt. People were very careful at the Boston Tea Party. They took the tea, but didn't hurt anyone.

7 I think Sam Adams was a great man. I don't agree with people who say he just tried to get attention. I think he really wanted to help people.

Now take the test on page 67.

Name ________________________ Date ____________

Test Strategy
Read the directions carefully. Make sure you understand what to do.

Read each item. Choose the best answer.

1 Which sentence is a fact?

- ⬭ Sam Adams was born in Boston.
- ⬭ I think that Sam was very smart.
- ⬭ Sam's plan for the Boston Tea Party was good.
- ⬭ Sam Adams is the most important person ever born in Massachusetts.

2 Which sentence is an opinion?

- ⬭ Sam Adams lived in Massachusetts.
- ⬭ Sam Adams planned the Boston Tea Party.
- ⬭ I think Sam Adams was very smart.
- ⬭ Some people decided to help Sam Adams.

3 Complete this sentence with a fact. Sam Adams—

- ⬭ was a great man.
- ⬭ wanted to break things.
- ⬭ was a leader of the American Revolution.
- ⬭ was the most important person in Boston.

4 Complete this sentence with an opinion. Sam Adams—

- ⬭ was a representative in the government of Massachusetts.
- ⬭ just tried to get attention.
- ⬭ knew many people in Boston.
- ⬭ planned the Boston Tea Party.

Name ______________________________ Date ______________

Vocabulary Skill

Idioms

Read the passage.

Rewrite the passage on a separate sheet of paper. Use an idiom to replace each underlined phrase.

Use the story and *English at Your Command!* pages 58–61 to find idioms.

After the twins returned from their vacation, they refused to tell me what they did at Grandma's house. They always kept talking about things that didn't matter. I started to feel very sad.

Finally, one twin said, "You have to promise not to tell our secret."

I said, "I agree!"

The other twin said, "We went back in time. We went to the Boston Tea Party."

I said, "That's ridiculous!"

The first twin said, "We'll be in trouble for telling you this. Grandma has a magic traveling hat. We really did dump tea in the harbor."

I got really mad. "Stop it!" I said. "Just forget it! Let's go play ball."

So we did. I never did find out what they did on that vacation.

MORE Idioms

Compare the two versions with a partner. Which version do you like better—the original or the one with idioms?

Name ______________________ Date ____________

Vocabulary: Key Words

Words from American History

Key Words
Congress
Constitution
declare
delegate
frontier
government
independent

Work with a partner.

Read each sentence.

Mark *T* for true. Mark *F* for false.

__F__ **1.** A **frontier** is an area of land where people have lived for a long time.

_____ **2.** The group of people who lead a country is called the **government**.

_____ **3.** The **Constitution** is the set of laws that the United States follows.

_____ **4.** An **independent** country is controlled by another country.

_____ **5.** Members of **Congress** make laws for the United States.

_____ **6.** When you **declare** something, you keep it a secret.

_____ **7.** A **delegate** is someone the people choose to speak and act for them.

MORE Key Words Practice

Rewrite each false statement above to make it true.

____

____

____

____

Name ______________________________ Date ______________

Grammar: Irregular Past Tense Verbs

Fourteen-Questions Game

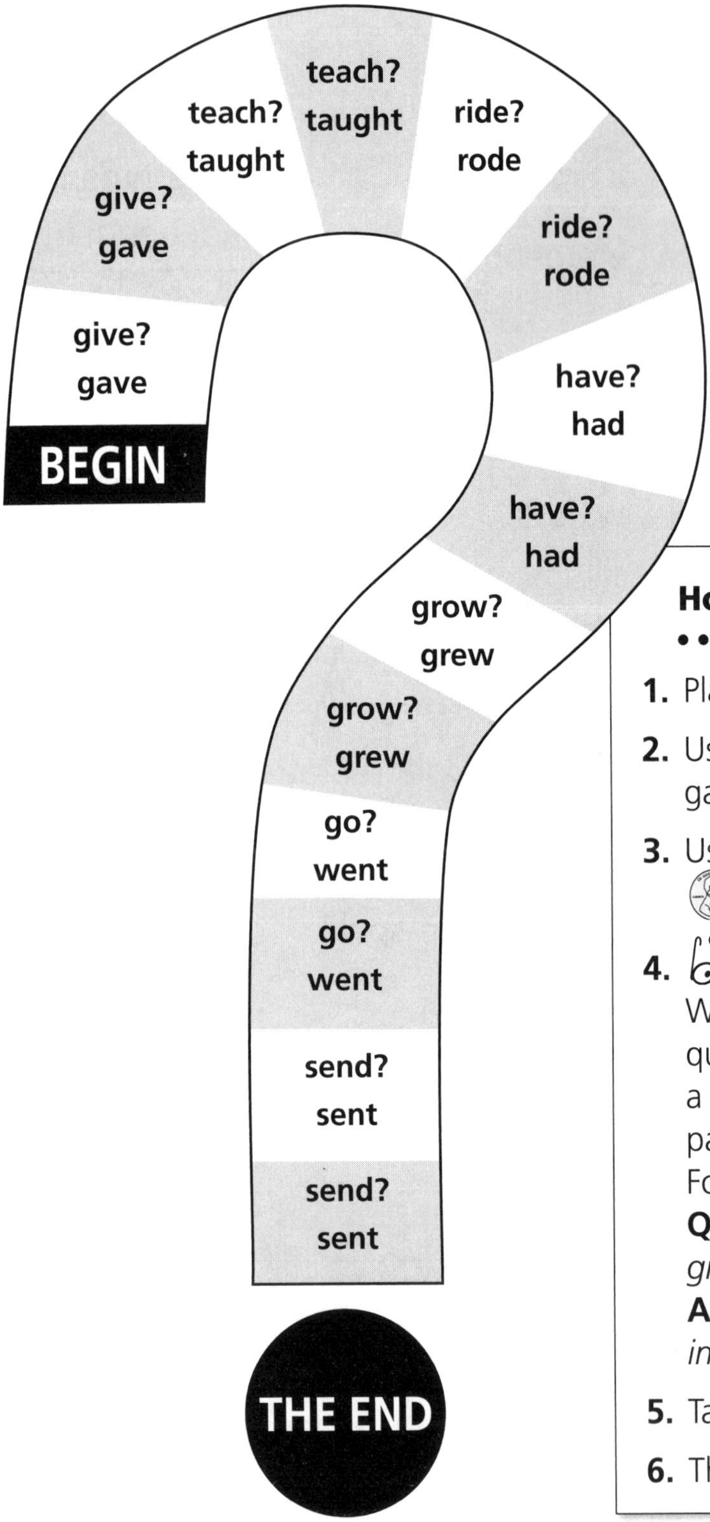

How to Play Fourteen Questions

1. Play with a partner.
2. Use an eraser or other small object as a game piece.
3. Use a coin to move.
   Heads = 1 space   Tails = 2 spaces
4. Look at the pictures in "George Washington." Find the verb with a question mark in your space. Use it to ask a question about a picture. Have your partner use the other verb to answer.
   For example:
   Question: *Where did George Washington grow up?*
   Answer: *George Washington grew up in Virginia.*
5. Take turns asking and answering questions.
6. The first one to reach **THE END** wins.

Name ______________________ Date ____________

Grammar: Irregular Past Tense Verbs

What Was George Really Like?

Read the journal entry.

Write the correct past tense form of the verb to complete each sentence.

Other Irregular Verbs

These action verbs have special forms to tell about the past.

Present Tense	fight	teach	become	find	take	get
Past Tense	fought	taught	became	found	took	got

Dear Journal,

George Washington ___got___ (get) a pony when he was a boy. That's when he started riding. His father __________ (teach) him. George __________ (become) a good rider. George's brother __________ (take) care of young George after their father died.

I want to know more about young George. I know he __________ (fight) in the American Revolution. But did he fight with his brothers and sisters? He __________ (become) a great man. I __________ (find) another book about him in the library. I checked it out and __________ (take) it home. I hope it tells me everything I want to know.

Name ____________________ Date ____________

Vocabulary Skill

Suffixes

Read the list of verbs.

Complete the chart.
Add the suffix *-ment, -tion,* or *-sion* to change each verb to a noun.

Check a dictionary to see which suffix to add and how the spelling changes.

Suffixes *-ment, -tion, -sion*

The suffixes ***-ment***, ***-tion***, and ***-sion*** change verbs into nouns.

Example:

Verb	+	Suffix	=	Noun
pay		**-ment**		**payment**

Verb	+	Suffix (*-ment, -tion,* or *-sion*)	=	Noun
1. retire	+	-ment	=	retirement
2. permit	+		=	
3. intend	+		=	
4. conclude	+		=	
5. measure	+		=	
6. correct	+		=	
7. attend	+		=	
8. accomplish	+		=	
9. move	+		=	
10. achieve	+		=	
11. discuss	+		=	
12. elect	+		=	

Name ____________ Date ____________

Graphic Organizer: Time Line

George Washington

Review "George Washington."

Complete the time line.

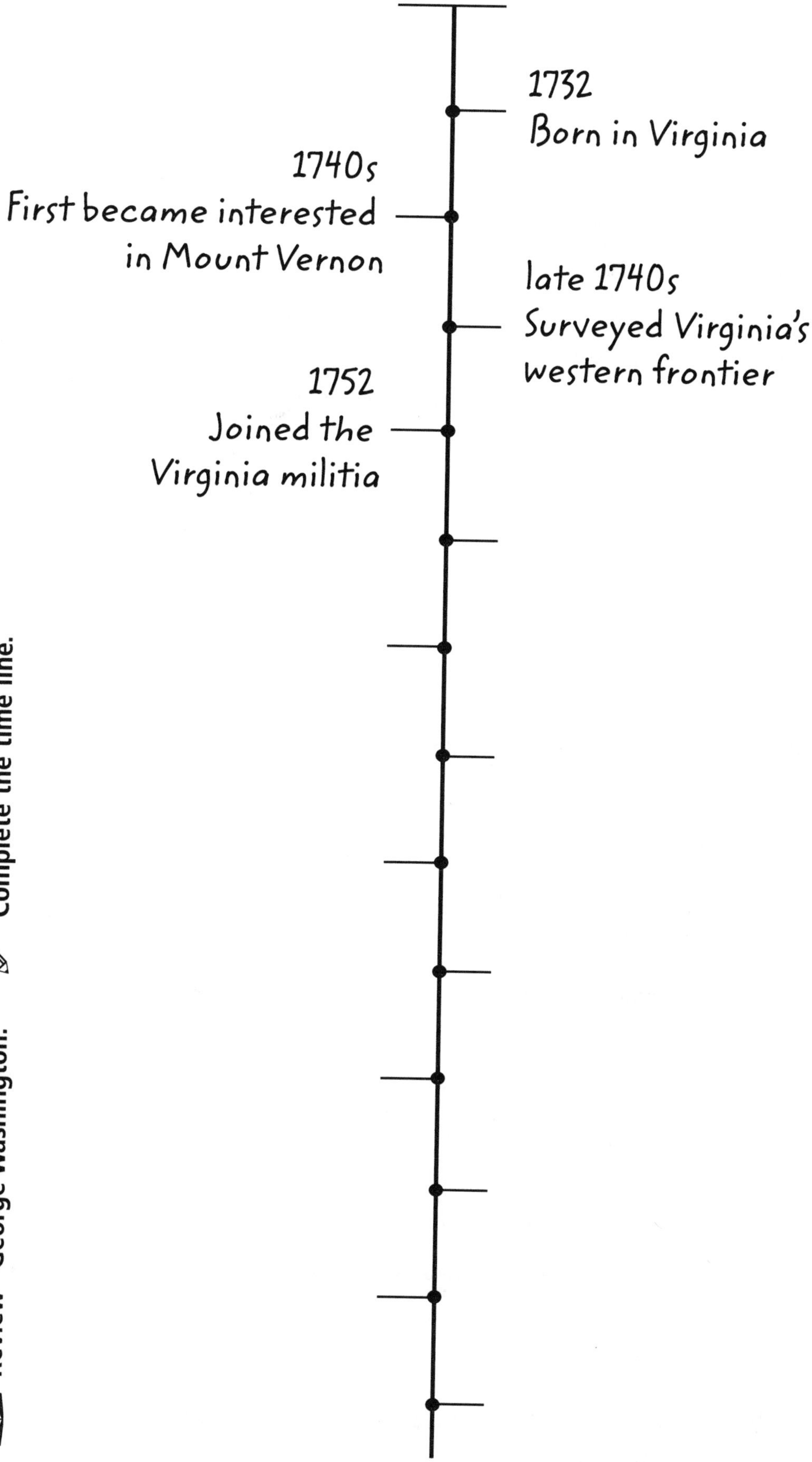

Name ______________________ Date ____________

Research Skill

Take Notes

How to Take Notes

- Write your research question at the top of a notecard.
- Write your source. List the title, author, and page number.
- Read the source. Look for information about your topic.
- Write down the information you find. Use your own words.

What was the Boston Massacre?
The Story of America by the
National Geographic Society,
pages 70–71
• A Boston crowd teased British soldiers.
• British soldiers shot their muskets.
• 5 colonists died.

Fill in the notecard using information from another book or a Web site.

Research question ➡

Title, author, and page number of your source ➡

Information ➡

MORE Notes

Get a blank index card or a sheet of paper. Write down a research fact from another book or another Web site.

Name ______________________ Date __________

Grammar: Past Tense Verbs

E-mail Sent!

Read the e-mail.

Write the correct past tense form of the verb to complete each sentence.

Past Tense Verbs

- Add ***-ed*** to most verbs to show that something happened in the past.
  clash → clash**ed**
- If the verb ends in **e**, drop the **e** before you add ***-ed***.
  decid~~e~~ → decid**ed**
- Some verbs have special forms for the past tense.
  fight → fought

Hi, Cleon,

I __decided__ (decide) to e-mail you the facts for our report. I ________ (find) some new books. I ________ (check) all my facts. I also ________ (send) an e-mail to Chan. Here is what I ________ (learn).

George Washington first ________ (become) President in 1789. He ________ (want) to stay on his farm, but his country ________ (need) him. So he ________ (go) to New York City. That was the capital then. He ________ (take) his oath of office there. He and Martha ________ (move) to New York. Later, they ________ (live) in Philadelphia.

I hope this helps.

Inés

Name ______________________________ Date ______________

Vocabulary Skill

Word Families

Read the passage. Underline 10 words with an affix.

Then complete the chart for five of the words you underlined.

Affixes and Their Meanings

Prefixes	Suffixes
anti- against	***-ent, -ence, -ment, -ation, -tion, -sion*** the state of
in-, ir-, il-, un- not	***-er, -or*** one who
pre- before	***-ful*** full of
re- again	***-ily, -ly*** in a ___ way
trans- across	***-less*** without

I want permission to go back in time. I want to return to the American Revolution. I'd like to see our government transform from a colony to a country. I'd like to hear Sam Adams's anti-British discussions. I'd like to see King George's endless interference in the affairs of the colonists. It was a time when it was unwise and illegal to talk openly about freedom. If we could all be visitors back then, we might recall where our Constitution came from. And we would proudly call the United States our home.

Word	Root Word	Affix	Meaning
permission	permit	-sion	the state of permitting

Name ____________________ Date ____________

Vocabulary: Key Words

Land and Water

Work with one or more partners.

Fill in the Venn diagram. Use Key Words and other words you know.

Key Words
canyon
coastline
dunes
geyser
landform
mountain range
waterfall

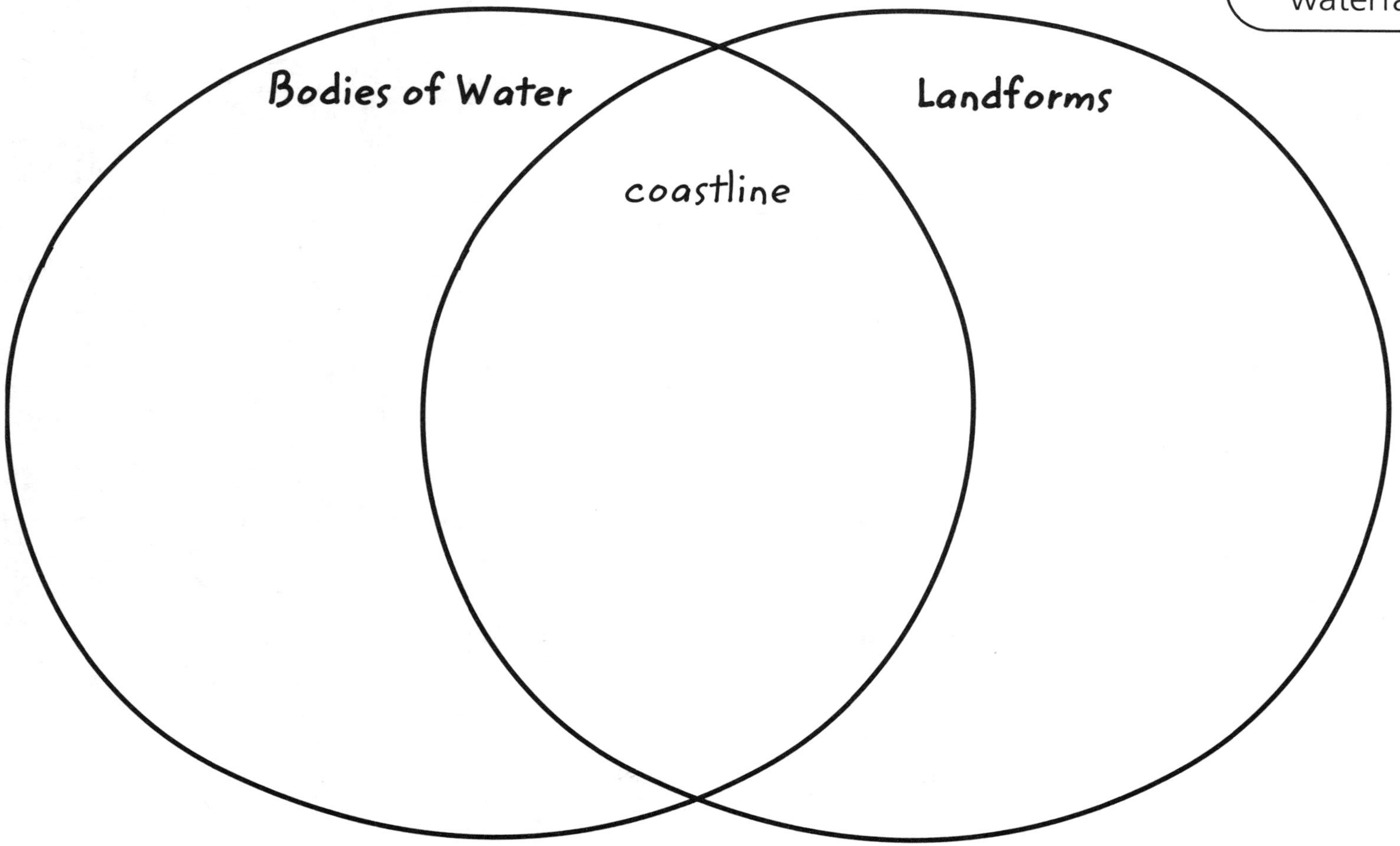

Name ______________________ Date ____________

Grammar: Descriptive Adjectives

Can You Describe It?

Adjectives for How Things Look		
shiny	large	big
long	great	small
deep	wide	

Look at the page in "Greetings from America."

Read each sentence on this page.

Write an adjective from the box to complete the sentence.

page 262 **1.** Cascades are waterfalls with a ___small___ volume of water.

page 262 **2.** Cascades often drop from ____________ heights.

page 262 **3.** They look like ____________ silver ribbons.

page 263 **4.** Horseshoe Falls is very ____________.

page 264 **5.** Ocean waves can pound ____________ holes into cliffs.

page 264 **6.** Some caves are ____________ enough to hold an entire town.

page 264 **7.** A cavern is a very, very ____________ cave.

page 265 **8.** In Mammoth Cave, you can see ____________ pillars.

Name ________________________ Date ____________

Grammar: Number and Order Words

Many People at the Beach

Look at the picture.

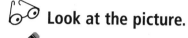

Write an adjective from the chart to complete each sentence.

Number and Order

Some **adjectives** tell "how many." Others tell "in what order."

Number (exact)	Number (not exact)	Order
one	some	first
two	several	second
three	many	third
four	few	fourth

It is the ____first____ day of summer. The seashore is a busy place.

Out at sea there are ____________ sailboats and ____________ motorboat.

Children are collecting ____________ seashells. There are ____________ waves. ____________ surfers are riding ____________ huge wave.

Oh, no! The ____________ surfer is falling off. At least the water is warm!

Name ______________________ Date __________

Grammar: Prepositions and Prepositional Phrases

Let's Walk up the Mountain!

- Look at the page in "Greetings from America."
- Read each sentence on this page.
- Complete the sentence with the correct word or words.
- Check your work with a partner.

Prepositional Phrases

Prepositions are short words like ***to***, ***in***, or ***of***. Prepositions are used with other words to make **prepositional phrases** that tell more about something.

Rest **by** the lake, then go **up** the mountain.

page 262 **1.** Water falls and crashes into a pool.
into a pool / **into** a field

page 263 **2.** People go ______________ in barrels.
over Niagara Falls / **over** Bryce Canyon

page 264 **3.** Water creates small cracks ______________.
of the rock / **in** the rock

page 264 **4.** Water flows ______________.
around the tunnels / **through** the tunnels

page 266 **5.** Wind can blow sand ______________.
after a valley / **across** a valley

page 268 **6.** The Rockies stretch ______________ to New Mexico.
from Florida / **from** Alaska

page 269 **7.** You can swim ______________.
in a lake / **between** a lake

page 270 **8.** Magma lies ______________.
until ground / **below** ground

MORE Prepositions

Write a paragraph to tell about your favorite place in "Greetings from America." Use prepositions.

Name ______________________________ Date ____________

Grammar: Adjectives That Compare

The Tallest Waterfall

Study the rules. Look at the pictures.

Complete the sentences. Add *-er* or *-est* to the word below the line.

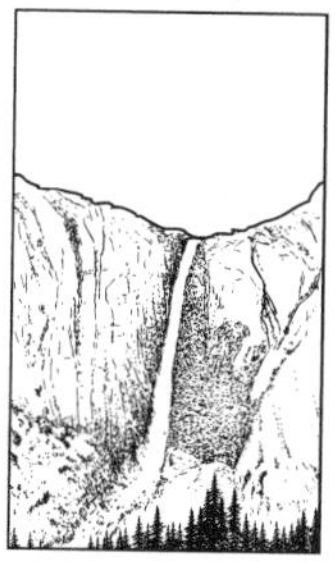

tall

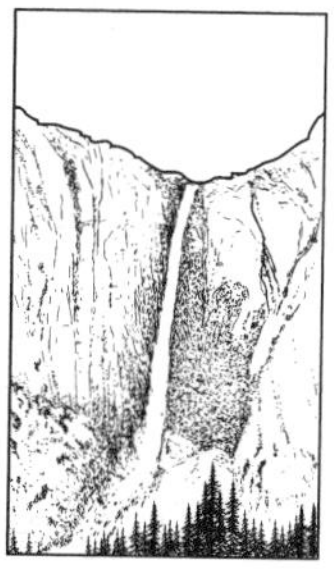

taller

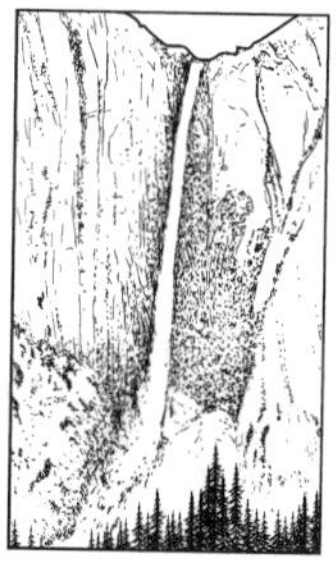

tallest

Rules for Comparing

- To compare two things, add ***-er***:

  Ribbon Falls is **taller** than Silver Strand Falls.

- To compare more than two things, add ***-est***:

  Ribbon Falls is the **tallest** waterfall in Yosemite National Park.

Ribbon Falls
1,612 feet

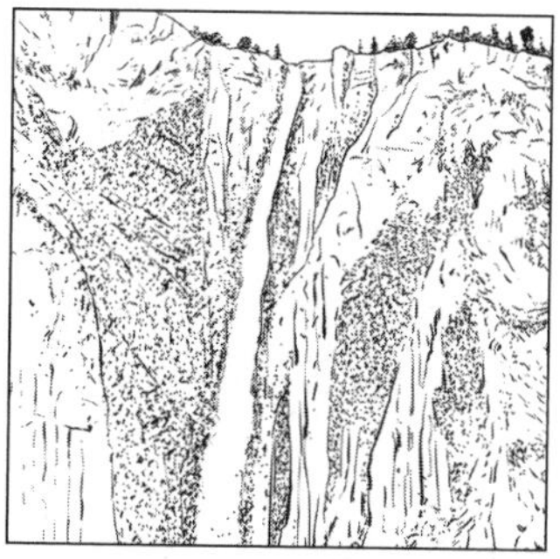

Vernal Falls
317 feet

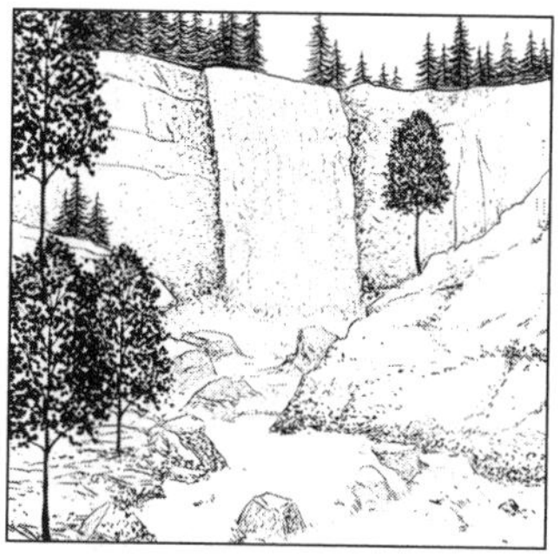

Silver Strand Falls
1,170 feet

Bridalveil Falls
620 feet

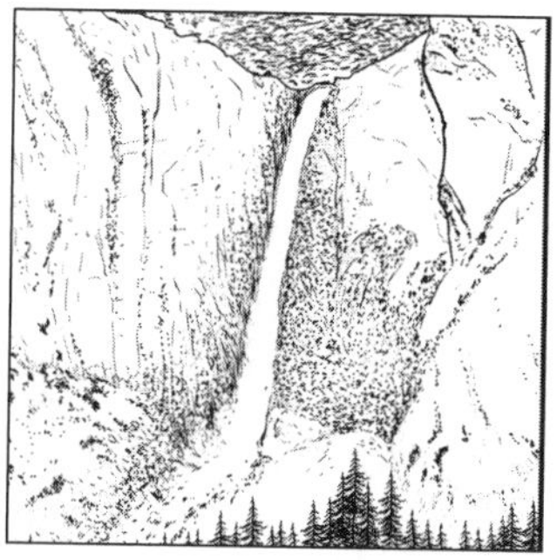

1. Ribbon Falls is ___taller___ than Bridalveil Falls.
(tall)

2. Silver Strand Falls is ______________ than Vernal Falls.
(tall)

3. Vernal Falls is the ______________ waterfall of all.
(short)

4. Bridalveil Falls is ______________ than Silver Strand Falls.
(short)

5. Ribbon Falls is the ______________ waterfall of all.
(tall)

Name ______________________ Date ____________

Grammar: Adjectives That Compare

Highest and Most Amazing

Read each sentence.

Write the correct form of the adjective.

Short and Long Adjectives

- For adjectives that are short words, add ***-er*** or ***-est*** to compare.

  high high**er** high**est**

- For adjectives that are long words, do not add ***-er*** or ***-est***. Use ***more*** or ***most*** instead.

  amazing **more** amazing **most** amazing

1. Pia has photos of the ______________ places.
   most amazing / amazingest
2. We talk about the places that are the ______________ of all.
   interestingest / most interesting
3. Yellowstone National Park is the ______________ national park.
   most old / oldest
4. Old Faithful is the ______________ geyser in Yellowstone.
   most famous / famousest
5. The Mojave Desert is the ______________ place in America.
   most low / lowest
6. The ______________ freshwater lake in the world is Lake Superior.
   largest / most large
7. The Mississippi River is ______________ than the Missouri River.
   more long / longer
8. I think the ______________ place to visit is New York City.
   most exciting / excitingest
9. Pia likes Colorado because the air is ______________ there.
   more clean / cleaner
10. Pia and I both want to visit Mount McKinley, in Alaska.
    It's the ______________ mountain in North America!
    tallest / most tall

Name ______________________ Date __________

Graphic Organizer: Main Idea Diagram

Greetings from America

Review "Greetings from America."

Complete the main idea diagram.

Main Idea	Details
Water and wind change things in nature.	Water erodes soft rock to form a waterfall in a river.
	Water makes cracks in limestone, and they get wider to form a cave or a cavern.

Name ______________________ Date ____________

Comprehension Skill

Read Long Words

Read the passage below. Think about how to read long words.

The Black Hills Caves

1 Hills are raised landforms like mountains, but hills aren't as tall as mountains.

2 The Black Hills are in South Dakota. They got their name because the pine trees on the hills make them look black. You can see some very interesting caves in the Black Hills.

3 Granite is in the core, or center, of the Black Hills. It is a type of rock. The granite has limestone rock around it. The limestone is prehistoric. It was created more than 300 million years ago on the floor of a very old sea. The caves were formed from this limestone.

4 First, small caves formed in the limestone. Then, the caves were covered by other layers of rock. The caves seemed to disappear.

5 Then, about 60 million years ago, the granite at the center of the Black Hills started to slowly push up. Rocks broke and fell.

6 When this happened, the limestone was lifted up, too. The limestone cracked, and pieces became disconnected. Water in the ground wore down the limestone, and the caves began to reappear. Later, the water ran out and the caves were left the way they look today.

7 The Black Hills caves are much older than other caves. Other layers of rock protect them. We must protect them, too, and not mistreat them. The Black Hills are a national treasure.

Now take the test on page 85.

Name ______________________ Date ____________

Test Strategy
Skip an item if you're not sure of the answer. Come back to it later. Make your best guess.

Read each item. Choose the best answer.

1 What does the word prehistoric mean?
- ⬭ not historic
- ⬭ before history was written down
- ⬭ incorrectly historic
- ⬭ without history

2 What does the word disconnected mean?
- ⬭ not connected
- ⬭ connected incorrectly
- ⬭ connected again
- ⬭ connected quickly

3 What does the word reappear mean?
- ⬭ to disappear again
- ⬭ to not appear
- ⬭ to appear again
- ⬭ to appear one time

4 What does the word mistreat mean?
- ⬭ to treat well
- ⬭ to treat badly
- ⬭ to treat carefully
- ⬭ to treat again

Name ______________________ Date ______________

Vocabulary: Key Words

A Very Big Word

Key Words
acre
enormous
gargantuan
gigantic
huge
mammoth
mighty
scenic

Work with a partner to complete the word wheel.

On each light section, write a word that means the same as the word in the middle.

On each shaded section, write a word that means the opposite.

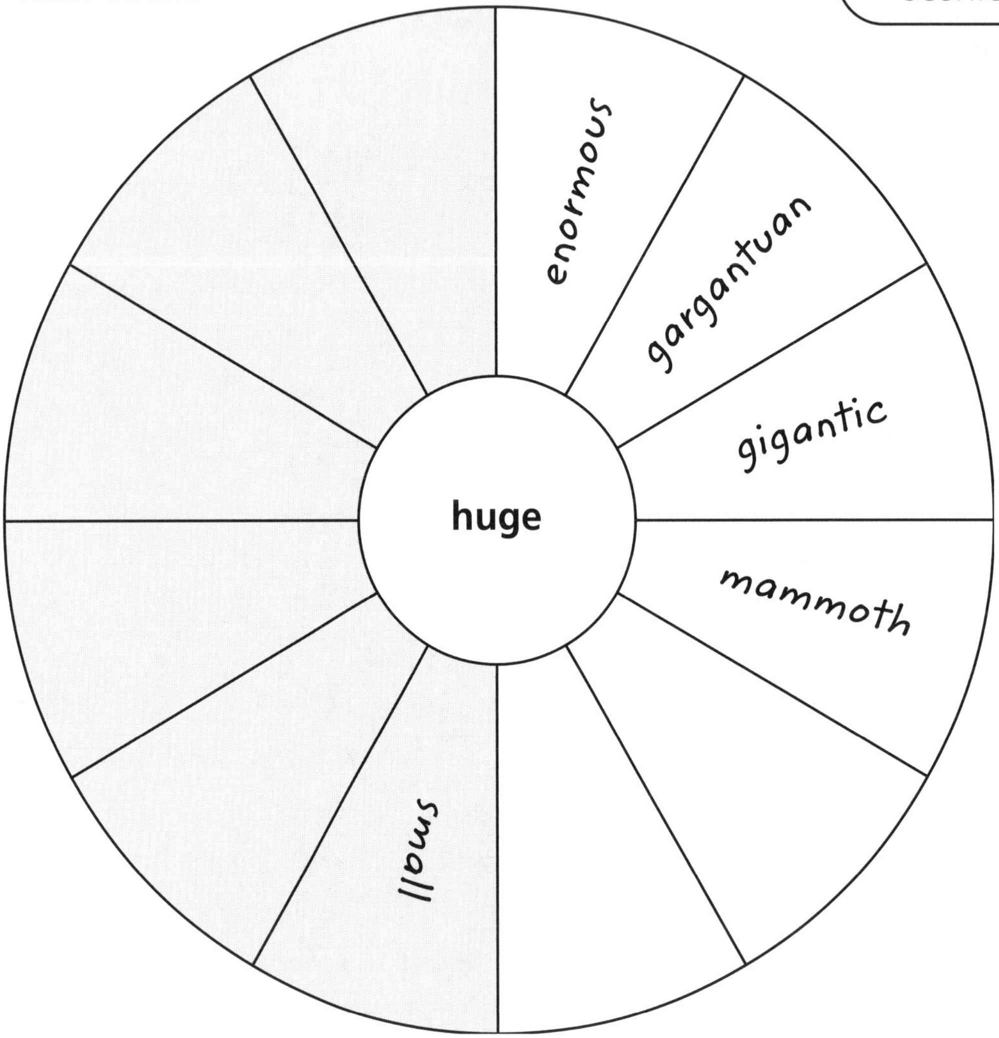

MORE Word Wheels

Work with a partner to make word wheels for ***mighty*** and ***scenic***. You can use a thesaurus or a dictionary.

Name ______________________ Date ______________

Grammar: Adverbs

Meet the Small Family

Read the paragraph.

Write an adverb in each blank. Choose an adverb from the box, or use one of your own.

> **Adverbs**
>
> Most **adverbs** tell more about a verb. They can tell how, where, or when. Adverbs that tell "how" often end in ***-ly***.
>
> A man planted a tree.
>
> Yesterday (when), a man carefully (how) planted a tree outside (where).

How		Where	When
carefully	happily	inside	then
busily	quietly	outside	always

The Small Family

The Smalls lived in a tree. They were so little, they almost always stayed ___inside___ (where). A squirrel had ______ (how) made a hole in the trunk. It was like a tiny cave. ______ (when) the squirrel moved away, and the Smalls moved in. The five Small children never went ______ (where). They played in the living room all day. Mr. Small ______ (how) made a table and seven chairs for them. Mrs. Small ______ (how) made them each a bed of soft leaves. They ______ (when) went to sleep when the first star came out. They slept ______ (how) all night until the sun came up.

Name ______________________ Date ______________

Grammar: Irregular Adjectives

The Best of the Best

Study the words in the box. Then read each sentence.

Write the correct form of the adjective.

Adjectives Chart

Some adjectives have special forms to compare.

good →	better →	best
bad →	worse →	worst
some →	more →	most
little →	less →	least

1. Tall tales are the ___best___ (best / most good) stories to read if you want to laugh.
2. Yesterday we read one in class. It was pretty good, but the one we read today was even ______________ (gooder / better).
3. I have ______________ (more little / less) interest in stories like "Cinderella."
4. My friend Pablo thinks the Paul Bunyan tales are the ______________ (most good / best) of all.
5. The ______________ (baddest / worst) idea of all is to argue about which story is the funniest.
6. Some tall tales are boring, but ______________ (somest / most) of them are pretty funny.
7. Nothing is ______________ (worse / badder) than a boring story!

MORE Comparisons

Get together with two partners. Compare movies or TV shows you have seen. Which are the best?

Name ______________________ Date __________

Graphic Organizer: Comparison Chart

The Bunyans

Review "The Bunyans." Complete the comparison chart.

How Were Landforms Made?

Landform	Tall Tale Explanation	Real Explanation
Mammoth Cave	Carrie lost her wishbone and dug for it.	Water dissolved the limestone rock.
Niagara Falls		
Bryce Canyon		
Great Sand Dunes		
Big Sur		
Continental Divide		
Old Faithful		

Name ______________________ Date ____________

Research Skill

Use an Index

Study this page from an index.

Then follow the directions on page 91.

Pages with pictures are in **boldface**.

Name ______________________ Date ____________

Research Skill

Use an Index

Write the answer to each question.

Use the index on page 90.

Check your work with a partner.

How to Use an Index

- Use alphabetical order to find a subject word.
- If details are listed under the main subject, find the best match.
- Jot down the page numbers. Skim those pages for the information you want.

1. On what pages would you find information on earthquakes?

   pages 32, 49, 107

2. Where would you find a picture of a desert ecosystem?

   ____

3. What do you think this book is about—insects or the Earth?

   ____

4. Where would you look to find information about farming?

   ____

5. Which animal would you find pictured on page 57?

   ____

6. If you want information about plant fossils, under what entry word would you look in the index?

   ____

7. On what pages would you find information about spring, summer, fall, or winter?

   ____

Name ______________________________ Date ______________

Grammar: Adjectives and Adverbs

Tell Me More!

Read the letter.

Rewrite the letter. Use adjectives and adverbs from the box (or use your own) to give more details.

Words to Add Details

- **Adjectives** tell about nouns.

What Kind	How Many
large	three
black	many
sunny	several

- **Adverbs** tell when, where, or how.

When	Where	How
soon	there	slowly
never	down	carelessly
yesterday	here	quickly

July 5, 2003

Dear Ana,

We rode on horses. It was a day. There were horses. My horse was a horse. We rode at first. Then we rode! At the end of the day, I returned. After riding a horse all day, I didn't want to sit.

Goodbye for now,
Julia

____

____

____

____

____

____

Name ____________________ Date __________

Vocabulary Skill

Figurative Language: Exaggeration

Use exaggeration to describe someone or something in a funny way.

Draw a picture that goes with your description.

Name ______________________ Date ____________

Vocabulary: Key Words

Words of Invention

Read each sentence.

Circle the correct Key Word. Then write the sentence.

Key Words
accomplish
discover
exhibit
experiment
invent
lightning
prove

1. I see ___lightning / exhibit___ flash in the night sky.

   I see lightning flash in the night sky.

2. I want to ___prove / invent___ machines that use that power.

   ____

3. I will do an ___exhibit / experiment___ to test each of my ideas.

   ____

4. The experiments can ___prove / invent___ that my ideas are correct.

   ____

5. Maybe I will ___discover / exhibit___ something new about electricity!

   ____

6. I will display my machines in a fancy ___experiment / exhibit___.

   ____

7. I want everyone to see the things that I ___accomplish / lightning___!

   ____

Name ______________________ Date ____________

Grammar: Subject and Predicate

Two Important Things

Read each sentence.

Put a line (/) between the subject and the predicate.

Then write the simple subject and the simple predicate.

1. We / have tickets for the museum.

   We have

2. The museum has a lot of exhibits.

   ____

3. My aunt from Texas got us the tickets.

   ____

4. My favorite exhibits are about electricity.

   ____

5. My little brother goes to the museum all the time.

   ____

6. He really loves the lightning machine.

   ____

Subject and Predicate

Every sentence has a **subject** and a **predicate**. The subject tells who or what the sentence is about. The predicate tells what the subject is, has, or does.

My older brother likes science a lot.

(My older brother = **subject**; likes science a lot. = **predicate**)

The most important word in the subject is the **simple subject**. The most important word in the predicate is the **simple predicate**. It is always the **verb**.

Simple subject: brother
Simple predicate: likes

MORE Subjects and Predicates

Make up a two-word sentence. **Example:** *Dog runs.*
Then ask a partner to make the sentence longer.
Example: *My dog Fuzzy runs at the beach on weekends.*

Name ______________________ Date ____________

Grammar: Compound Predicates

Study and Learn

Read each pair of sentences.

Combine the sentences to write one longer sentence.

Two into One

When two sentences have the same subject, you can combine them. The result is one longer sentence with a **compound predicate**.

Gary **sings**. Gary **plays the guitar**.
Gary **sings and plays the guitar**.

1. Sam watches TV. Sam waits for his sister Kara.

   Sam watches TV and waits for his sister Kara.

2. They go outside. They walk to the museum.

   ____

3. Terri visits the museum. Terri meets Sam and Kara there.

   ____

4. Kara studies the exhibits. Kara learns about electricity.

   ____

5. She writes a report. She shares it with her class.

   ____

6. The students listen to the report. The students ask questions.

   ____

MORE Compound Predicates

Write two sentences with the same subject. Use a different verb in each sentence.

Have a partner combine the sentences into one sentence that has a compound predicate.

Name ______________________________ Date ______________

Grammar: Compound Subject

You and I Can Learn Together!

Read each sentence.

Write the correct verb to complete the sentence.

What Verb Do I Use?

When ***and*** joins two simple subjects, use a verb that tells about more than one.

Ellen and John **walk** to the museum.

When ***or*** joins the subjects, use a verb that agrees with the simple subject closest to it.

My parents or my uncle **gives** them a ride after school.

1. Katrina and her family ___are___ (is / are) at a museum.
2. She and her sister ______________ (wants / want) to learn about Ben Franklin.
3. Katrina hopes that films or an exhibit ______________ (shows / show) Franklin's inventions.
4. Mrs. Faber and her family ______________ (read / reads) about all of the inventions.
5. The lightning rod or bifocals ______________ (is / are) Franklin's greatest invention.
6. Mrs. Faber, Mr. Faber, and Carla ______________ (walk / walks) to different exhibits.
7. Katrina and Ben ______________ (go / goes) back to his workshop.
8. Ben and William ______________ (has / have) a kite.
9. Ben and his son ______________ (prove / proves) that lightning is electricity.
10. Katrina's family and friends ______________ (is / are) not going to believe what happened!

Name ______________________ Date __________

Vocabulary Skill

Homophones

Read each sentence.

Circle the correct spelling. Then write the sentence.

1. Ben Franklin picked the ___ (right) / write ___ time to do his experiment.

   Ben Franklin picked the right time to do his experiment.

2. The wind ___ blue / blew ___ Ben's kite high up in the sky.

   ____

3. Katrina got to ___ see / sea ___ the lightning strike the wire.

   ____

4. She was happy to ___ bee / be ___ there for that exciting moment.

   ____

5. Later, Ben had a gift ___ four / for ___ Katrina.

   ____

6. He gave her ___ one / won ___ penny.

   ____

7. A penny is one ___ sent / cent ___.

   ____

8. You need a lot of pennies to ___ by / buy ___ anything today!

   ____

Name ______________________ Date ______________

Graphic Organizer: Venn Diagram

Ben Franklin's Experiment

Review "Ben Franklin's Experiment."

Complete the Venn diagram.

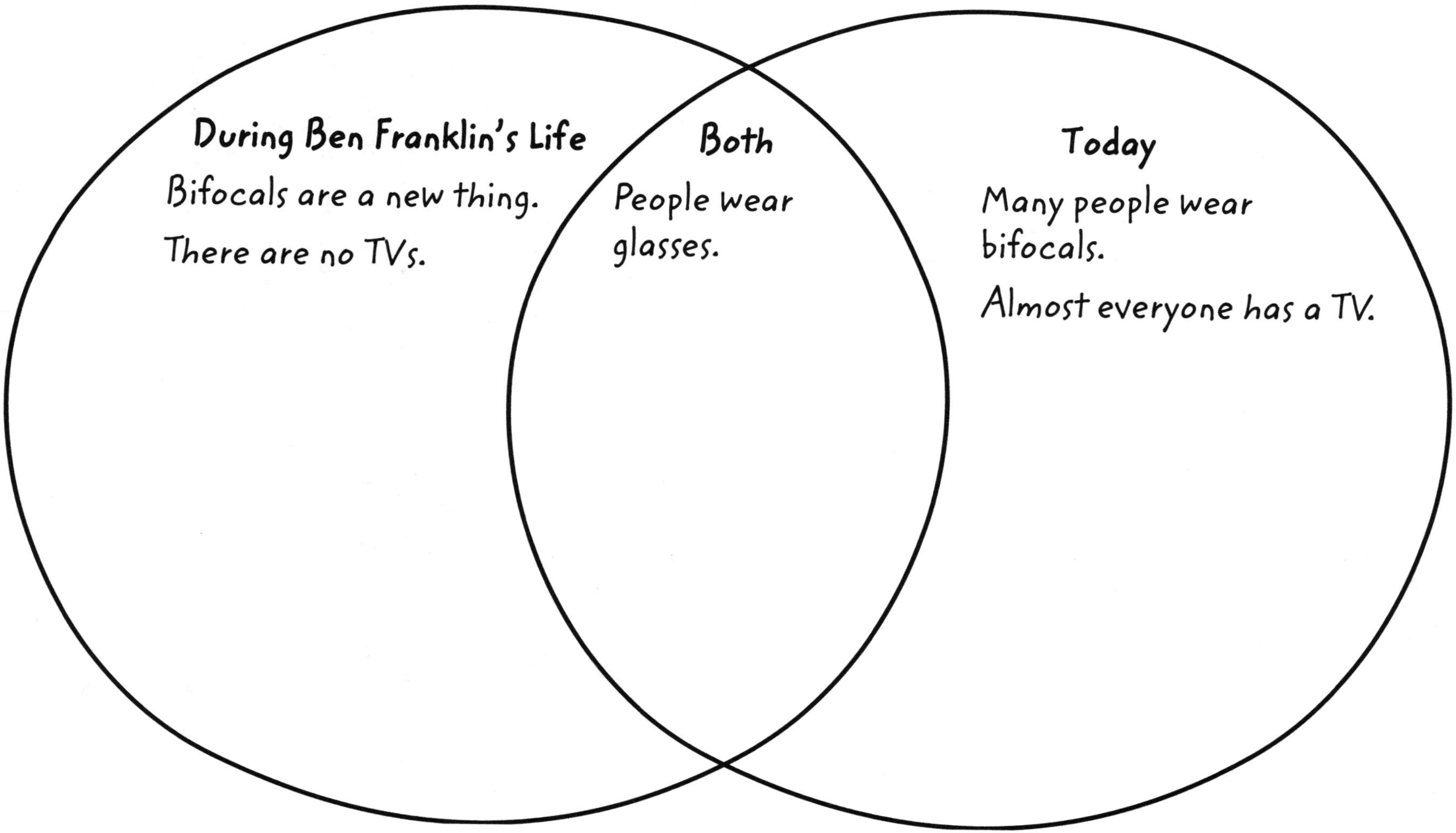

During Ben Franklin's Life
Bifocals are a new thing.
There are no TVs.
Both
People wear glasses.
Today
Many people wear bifocals.
Almost everyone has a TV.

Name ______________________ Date ____________

Comprehension Skill

Summarize

Read the passage below. Think about how to summarize it.

The Light Bulb

1 **Narrator:** Thomas Alva Edison invented the electric light bulb that we use in lamps. Listen to Harriet as she talks to Mr. Edison in her dream.

2 **Harriet:** Why did you want to invent the light bulb?

3 **Edison:** Before electric light bulbs, we used gas for our lights. Gas came through pipes in houses. The gas was lit and the flame gave off light. The burning gas was dirty, and bad to breathe. The dirt from the burning gas covered the walls, furniture, and floors. Sometimes the gas even caused house fires and explosions.

4 **Narrator:** Electricity changed all that. Many of the things we use today, such as refrigerators, fans, and computers, would not work without electricity. It all started with the invention of the electric light bulb!

5 **Harriet:** Did you work for a long time on your invention?

6 **Edison:** Oh, yes, I did! I worked hard, and I never gave up. I did 1,200 experiments before I made a light bulb that would give light for two days. Later, I made a bulb that could glow for more than 1,200 hours! When I did my experiments, I worked very long hours. I only got about three or four hours of sleep each night!

7 **Harriet:** I'm glad you never gave up. Because of your invention, we now have safe lighting in our homes. We also have streetlights, and lights in cars. We have lights that let us see the world at night. Our lives would be very different without light bulbs!

Now take the test on page 101.

Name ______________________________ Date ______________

Test Strategy
Look for key words like *belongs* and *best*. They will help you find the correct answer.

Read each item. Choose the best answer.

1 Which sentence belongs in a summary of paragraph 3 on page 100?

- ⊂⊃ Gas lights made houses dirty and were not safe to use.
- ⊂⊃ Gas came through pipes.
- ⊂⊃ Gas was lit.
- ⊂⊃ Burning gas made floors dirty.

2 Which sentence belongs in a summary of paragraph 6 on page 100?

- ⊂⊃ Edison liked to do experiments.
- ⊂⊃ Light bulbs changed our lives.
- ⊂⊃ Edison did not need much sleep.
- ⊂⊃ Edison worked hard on his invention.

3 Which of the following is the best summary of the whole article?

- ⊂⊃ Because of light bulbs we have many new things, like refrigerators, fans, lamps, and car lights.
- ⊂⊃ Edison got three or four hours of sleep every night. He made a bulb that could glow for more than 1,200 hours.
- ⊂⊃ Edison worked hard to invent the electric light bulb. Electric lights are safer than gas lights. Light bulbs have changed the way we live.
- ⊂⊃ Gas light was dirty. It made houses dirty, and people breathed in the dirt. Electric lights are much cleaner.

Name ________________________________ Date ______________

Vocabulary Skill

Nonliteral Language

Read the paragraph. Notice the underlined idioms and phrases.

Rewrite the paragraph. Use your own words to replace the underlined words.

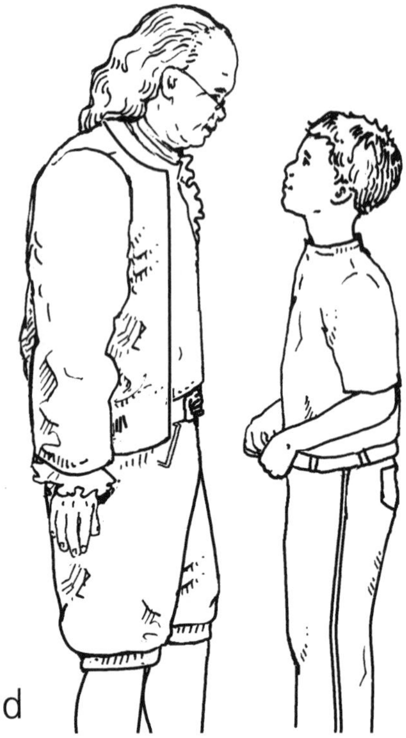

Katrina said that Ben Franklin might turn up again. "You could meet him," she said. "Do you think that would be fun?" I said, "You bet!" I look forward to meeting him. I hope she is not pulling my leg. I asked her how Ben could travel through time. She said time travel is a piece of cake for him. She said that Ben is smart as a whip and can do anything. He taught her to never give up, even if things seem hard. He said hard work helps you get ahead in life. I agree. I always put my best foot forward! I'm glad that Ben Franklin and I see eye to eye.

Katrina said that Ben Franklin might appear again.

Name ______________________ Date ____________

Vocabulary: Key Words

Energy Words

Key Words
atom
circuit
electron
energy
magnet

Write a Key Word to complete each sentence.

1. An ___atom___ is the smallest part of something.
2. An ______________ is part of an atom.
3. A ______________ can cause electrons to move in a wire.
4. The moving electrons are electricity. Electricity travels in a path called a ______________.
5. Electricity gives us ______________ to use TVs, lights, and many other things.

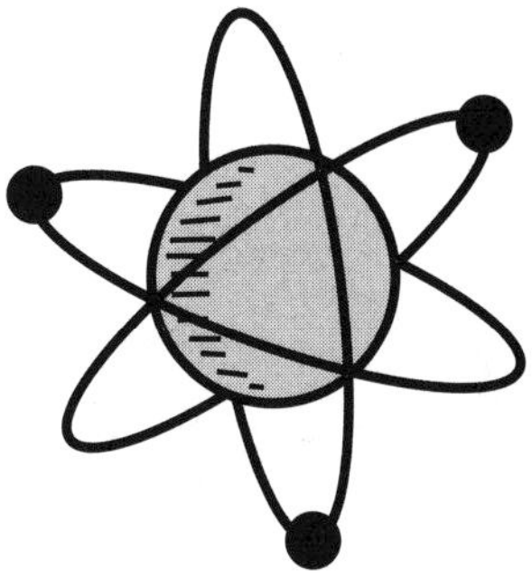

Read each sentence.

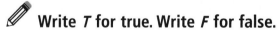

Write *T* for true. Write *F* for false.

__F__ 6. Some things are not made of atoms.

_____ 7. An electron makes a magnet move.

_____ 8. A magnet can attract metal.

_____ 9. A circuit is a light bulb.

_____ 10. Electricity is a form of energy.

Name ______________________ Date ____________

Grammar: Compound Sentences

Electricity, Energy, and Power

Read each pair of sentences.

Combine the two sentences using *and*, *but*, or *or*.

Combine Sentences

- Use ***and*** to join ideas that are alike.
  I turn on the lamp, **and** light fills the room.
- Use ***but*** to put together ideas that show a difference.
  I turned on the switch, **but** the lamp didn't work.
- Use ***or*** to show a choice between ideas.
  Fix the lamp, **or** get a new one.
- Use a comma before ***and***, ***but***, or ***or***.

1. Electricity helps us a lot. Life would be hard without it.

Electricity helps us a lot, and life would be hard without it.

2. Many machines use electricity. Some use gas.

____

____

3. Machines help us do work. They make our lives easier.

____

____

4. Your energy comes from food. Electrical energy has to be made.

____

____

5. You can use electricity. You can try to live without it!

____

____

Name ______________________ Date ____________

Vocabulary Skill

Multiple-Meaning Words

Read each sentence. Then read both meanings of the underlined word.

Circle the letter of the correct meaning. Write the clues that helped you choose the meaning.

1. A magnet pulls the electrons. Electrons speed from atom to atom.

A. How fast something is moving. *noun*

(B.) To move fast. *verb*

"Speed" is in the predicate. It is a verb that tells what electrons do.

2. This creates the flow of electricity.

A. To move in a current or stream. *verb*

B. Movement in a current or stream. *noun*

____

3. Generators with big magnets supply electricity to your city.

A. To give. *verb*

B. The amount of something there is to use. *noun*

____

4. When you switch a light on, you use electricity from generators.

A. Something that opens or closes an electric circuit. *noun*

B. To turn a light or electric machine on or off. *verb*

____

Name ______________________ Date ____________

Grammar: Modals

The Make-a-Sentence Game

How to Play The Make-a-Sentence Game

1. Play with a partner.
2. Spin the spinner for the beginning of a sentence.
3. Finish the sentence.

   No one should climb a tree near power lines.

4. Write your sentence on a sheet of paper.
5. Read your sentence to your partner.
6. Take turns. See how many sentences you and your partner can write in 15 minutes!

Make a Spinner

1. Get a brad and a large paper clip.
2. Push the brad through the center of the circle.

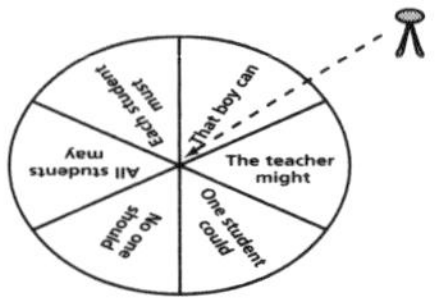

3. Open the brad.

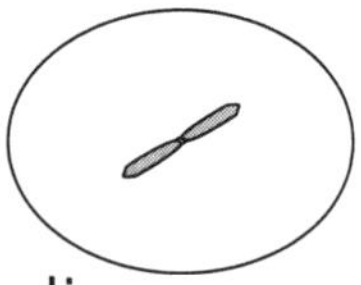

4. Hook the paper clip over the brad to make a spinner.

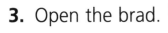

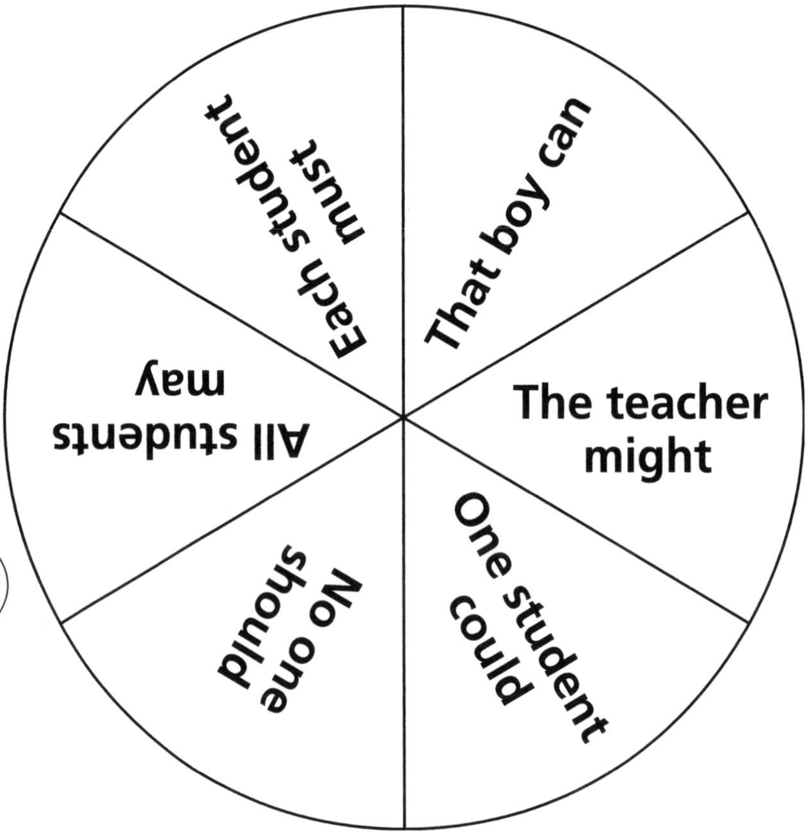

Name ______________________ Date __________

Vocabulary Skill

Content Area Words

Choose a content area word from "Switch On, Switch Off" or from another article or report.

Complete the card to tell about the word.

Share the card with your classmates.

Word: ______________________

Content area: ______________________

How the word is used: ______________________

____

Sample sentence: ______________________

____

____

Drawing or diagram:

Name ______________________ Date __________

Grammar: Compound Sentences

They Go Together!

Read each pair of sentences.

Combine the two sentences using *and*, *but*, or *or*.

Combine Sentences

- Use ***and*** to join ideas that are alike.
- Use ***but*** to put together ideas that show a difference.
- Use ***or*** for a choice between ideas.
- Use a comma before ***and***, ***but***, or ***or***.

1. Machines help us do work. We should be thankful for them.

Machines help us do work, and we should be thankful for them.

2. Some machines save energy. Other machines waste it.

____

____

3. You can choose the right machine. You can choose the wrong one.

____

____

4. My family has a new washing machine. It saves energy.

____

____

5. We can wash clothes in the machine. We can wash them by hand.

____

____

6. We use a lot of other machines at home. I'm glad we have them.

____

____

Name ______________________ Date ____________

Graphic Organizer: Cause-and-Effect Chart

Switch On, Switch Off

Review "Switch On, Switch Off."

Complete the cause-and-effect chart.

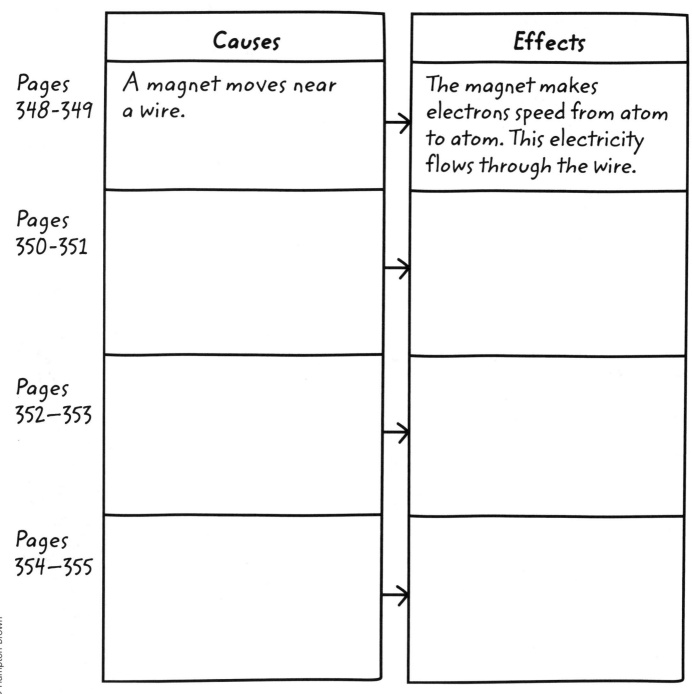

	Causes		Effects
Pages 348–349	A magnet moves near a wire.	→	The magnet makes electrons speed from atom to atom. This electricity flows through the wire.
Pages 350–351		→	
Pages 352–353		→	
Pages 354–355		→	

Name ______________________ Date ____________

Respond to Literature

It's Electric!

What is the most interesting fact you learned about electricity in "Switch On, Switch Off"?

Write a paragraph. Tell the fact and why it is interesting to you.

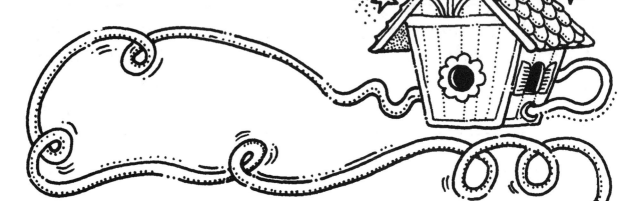

Name ______________________ Date ____________

Grammar: Helping Verbs

You Might Be Shocked!

Look at each picture. Read the sentence.

Write a helping verb from the box to complete each sentence.

Helping Verbs		
can	may	might
could	must	should

1.  Stop! You ______________ never touch electrical devices when you are wet.

2.  You ______________ stay indoors during a lightning storm.

3.  You ______________ never use an electrical device with a damaged cord.

4. 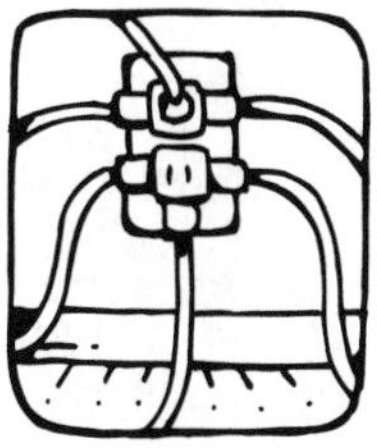 Do not overload outlets. It ______________ start a fire.

5.  You ______________ not go near fallen power lines.

Name ______________________ Date __________

Research Skill

Use a Glossary

Study this glossary.

Then follow the directions on page 113.

Glossary for "Switch On, Switch Off"

atom (**a**-tum) *noun* [Greek *atomos*: that cannot be divided] An **atom** is the smallest part of a substance. Everything in the world is made of atoms.

current (**kur**-unt) *noun* The **current** is the movement or flow of electricity.

electric (i-**lek**-trik) *adjective* 1. Having to do with electricity. 2. Powered by electricity: *We have an electric oven.*

electron (i-**lek**-tron) *noun* An **electron** is a part of an atom. The flow of electrons in a wire creates electricity.

energy (**en**-ur-jē) *noun* [Greek *energeia*: activity] **Energy** is the power to do work.

outlet (**owt**-let) *noun* An **outlet** is a place in a circuit where you can get electricity by putting in a plug. Houses usually have outlets on their walls.

plug (plug) *noun* A **plug** is the part at the end of an electric cord with two or three metal prongs through which electricity can flow.

power plant (**pow**-ur plant) *noun* A **power plant** is a building where electricity is made.

Name ______________________ Date ____________

Research Skill

Use a Glossary

Use the glossary on page 112 to answer each question.

1. Where is electricity made? at a power plant
2. What word is used for the flow of electricity? ____________
3. Where in a house can you usually find outlets? ____________
4. What do you call a toothbrush that uses electricity? ____________
5. Where does the word ***atom*** come from? ____________
6. What parts of atoms move to create electricity? ____________

Write an entry word from the glossary on page 112 to complete each sentence.

7. A plug is part of an electric cord.
8. You need ____________ to do work.
9. To use an ____________ fan, put its plug into an outlet.
10. Electricity moves in a ____________.
11. The origin of the word ____________ is the Greek word ***energeia***.
12. The only entry in this glossary that is an adjective is

____________.

Name ______________________________ Date ______________

Vocabulary: Key Words

Freedom Words

Work with a partner.

On separate sheets of paper, make a definition map for each Key Word. Follow the examples and instructions of the definition map for "conversation."

Key Words
conversation
determined
favorite
protection
public
special
welcoming

Write the Key Word in this section.

Here, write **examples** of the Key Word, or words that mean the **same** as the Key Word.

conversation	talk chat discussion when I talk to my friends
argument fight silence when my sister screams at me	A conversation is when you talk to people in a nice way.

Here, write things that are **not** examples of the Key Word, or words that mean the **opposite**.

In this section, write a definition in your own words.

Name ______________________ Date ______________

Grammar: Present Progressive Tense

At the Library

Look at each picture.

Write *am, is,* or *are* plus the *-ing* form of the verb to complete each sentence.

Helping Verbs

The helping verb always agrees with the subject.

Subject	Verb
I	am
he, she, it	is
we, you, they	are

1. The boys ___are going___ to the library.
go

2. The woman ______________ a book.
read

3. I ______________ a letter to the mayor.
write

4. Little Nicky ______________ a picture.
draw

5. The boys ______________ a lot of books.
carry

Name ________________________ Date ____________

Grammar: Future Tense

What Will You Do?

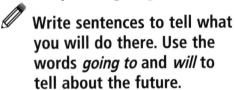

Work with a partner.

Look at the picture of the library. Imagine that you and your partner are planning to go there.

Write sentences to tell what you will do there. Use the words *going to* and *will* to tell about the future.

1. We are going to find lots of books in the library.
2. ____________________
3. ____________________
4. ____________________
5. ____________________
6. ____________________
7. ____________________
8. ____________________

MORE Future Tense Verbs

Will you go someplace special with your family this year? What will you see and do there?

Write about the place. Use words that tell about the future.

Name ______________________________ Date ____________

Literary Analysis

Character's Point of View

Think of a story you have read, or a movie you have seen. Think of a character that was NOT the main character. How do you think that character thought or felt?

Write the title of the story and the name of the character. Then tell the story from that character's point of view.

Story or Movie ______________________________

Character ______________________________

What the Character Thinks ______________________________

Name ______________________ Date ____________

Grammar: Future Tense

I Won't Forget!

Review the page in "Goin' Someplace Special."

Read the sentence on this page.

Change the underlined words to a contraction.

Contractions with *Will*

- Form a contraction with a **pronoun** plus ***will*** like this:

  I + ~~wi~~ll = I'll
  he + ~~wi~~ll = he'll

- Form a contraction with ***will*** plus ***not*** like this:

  will + not = won't

page 378 1. Mama Frances said, "I trust <u>you will</u> be particular."

Mama Frances said, "I trust you'll be particular."

page 383 2. <u>I will</u> give Mrs. Grannell my seat on the bus.

____

page 388 3. We <u>will not</u> eat at Monroe's Restaurant.

____

page 391 4. <u>She will</u> be pushed into the hotel.

____

page 392 5. The man is angry. <u>He will</u> tell her to leave.

____

page 398 6. They <u>will not</u> let her sit downstairs at the theater.

____

page 400 7. <u>It will</u> be good to go in the library.

____

page 400 8. She <u>will not</u> stop until she gets there.

____

Name ______________________ Date ____________

Graphic Organizer: Goal-and-Outcome Map

Goin' Someplace Special

Review "Goin' Someplace Special."

Complete the story map.

Goal

'Tricia Ann wants to go to the library alone.

Obstacles

1. 'Tricia Ann is not happy because she has to sit in the back of the bus.
2.
3.

Turning Point

Outcome

Name ______________________ Date ____________

Comprehension Skill

Make Predictions

Read the passage below. Think about how to make predictions.

Nine Children in Little Rock

1 In 1957, Elizabeth was a young girl in Little Rock, Arkansas. She was going to go to a new school. "Why don't the white people want me in that school?" she asked her mother.

2 Her mother looked at Elizabeth and said, "Before, only white children could go to that school. But the government passed a law. It says people of all colors can go to the same school."

3 The next morning, Elizabeth went to the school. She and her friends were the only black children. They were nine children who felt alone.

4 People asked questions and took pictures. Then Elizabeth saw a group of people near the steps of the school. They were angry. Elizabeth and her friends got closer. They heard the people say mean things about them.

5 The children all held hands. Elizabeth looked straight ahead and walked up to the school. When they went in the school, the people outside yelled at them.

6 In the classroom, the other students stared at her. A few children seemed friendly, but they didn't talk to her.

7 When she got home, Elizabeth cried. She said she never wanted to see that school again. Her mother said, "You don't have to go back if you don't want to."

8 But that night, Elizabeth surprised her mother. She said, "I'm afraid, but the law says I can be there. I'll go back tomorrow."

Now take the test on page 121.

Name ______________________ Date ____________

Test Strategy
Check your answers if you have time. Reread the questions and the answers you marked.

Read each item. Choose the best answer.

1 Read paragraphs 1 to 3 on page 120 again. What clue helps you predict that some people at the school will be mean to Elizabeth?

- ⬭ Elizabeth went to a new school.
- ⬭ Elizabeth's mother looked at her.
- ⬭ Elizabeth was a young girl in Little Rock.
- ⬭ Elizabeth asked, "Why don't the white people want me in that school?"

2 Read paragraph 4 on page 120. Think about Elizabeth's first day at school. What do you think will happen when Elizabeth goes back to the school the next day?

- ⬭ Everyone will smile at her.
- ⬭ She will be late for school.
- ⬭ Some people will still be angry.
- ⬭ All the children will want to be her friend.

3 How do you think Elizabeth's mother will feel if Elizabeth keeps going to the new school?

- ⬭ She will be angry.
- ⬭ She will be proud of her daughter.
- ⬭ She won't care.
- ⬭ She will feel sad.

Name ______________________ Date ____________

Literary Analysis

How Characters Change

Think about characters from other stories you know.

Complete the chart. Tell how each character feels in each part of the story. Tell why the character's feelings change.

Character/Story	Beginning	Middle	End

Name ______________________ Date ____________

Vocabulary: Key Words

Friendship Words

Think of a good friend you have or would like to have.

Complete each sentence using your own words.

Key Words
compromise
encourage
inspire
make a difference
partnership
respect

1. My friend and I have a good **partnership** because we ______________________

____

2. I have a lot of **respect** for my friend because ______________________

____

3. I **encourage** my friend to ______________________

____

4. My friend **inspires** me to ______________________

____

5. My friend **makes a difference** in my life because ______________________

____

6. It's better to reach a **compromise** than to fight when we don't agree, because ______________________

____

Name ______________________ Date ____________

Grammar: Complex Sentences

Two into One

Combine the two sentences into one sentence using *because* or *when*.

1. I went to the library. I had to do research.

   I went to the library because I had to do research.

2. I tried to go inside. The door would not open.

   ____

3. I went home. My mother asked me what was wrong.

   ____

4. I was angry. The library was closed.

   ____

5. I studied for a long time. I had a lot of homework.

   ____

6. I finished my homework. I went to sleep.

   ____

Name ______________________ Date ____________

Grammar: Complex Sentences

I Go to the Library

Complete each sentence using your own words.

1. If I want a special book, I go to the library.
2. I ask the librarian for help if ______________________.
3. If ______________________, I can find the book quickly.
4. If ______________________, I look for another book to read.
5. If ______________________, I help my friend find a book.
6. If ______________________, we meet at the library.
7. We do better work if ______________________.
8. I'll see my friend again soon if ______________________.

MORE Complex Sentences

Work with a partner.

Write more sentences about the library using *if*. Each partner can give one part of each sentence.

Name ______________________ Date ______________

Vocabulary Skill

Content Area Words

Find the word on the page in "Getting to Someplace Special."

Write the meaning. Then find out what the word means in a different content area. Write that meaning.

Check your answers with a partner.

Word	Social Studies Meaning	Meaning in Different Content Area
sign page 412	a board with a message that is put up in a public place	**Math:** a symbol, such as + or −
marine page 415		**Science:**
project page 414		**Science:**
culture page 423		**Science:**

Name ______________________ Date __________

Graphic Organizer: Summary Chart

Getting to Someplace Special

Review "Getting to Someplace Special."

Complete the chart.

Pages	Summary
412–413	The McKissacks love to read. When they were children, they went to the library often.
414–415	
416–417	
418–419	
420–422	
423	

Name ______________________ Date ____________

Respond to Literature

My Own Experience

Patricia McKissack used experiences from her childhood to create the character 'Tricia Ann and the fictional events in "Goin' Someplace Special."

Write about an experience from your life that you might want to turn into a story someday.

Name ______________________ Date ____________

Grammar: Join Sentences

They Go Together

Work with a partner.

Read the two sentences.

Put the sentences together to make one sentence. Use the conjunction *when, if,* or *because*.

1. I met Yao. We decided to create stories together.

   When I met Yao, we decided to create stories together.

2. I am happy I met Yao. He is a great partner.

   ____

   ____

3. Yao has finished gathering information. I turn it into a story.

   ____

   ____

4. He doesn't give me enough information. I ask him to do more research.

   ____

   ____

5. We work hard on our stories. We want them to be really good.

   ____

   ____

Name ______________________________ Date ______________

Vocabulary: Key Words

A Migrant Family

Key Words
camp
harvest
migrant
move on
settle down

Write a Key Word to complete each sentence.

1. We are ______________ workers from Mexico.
2. We live in a ______________ near the fields.
3. When the crops are ready, we ______________ them.
4. After that, we ______________ to another place.
5. We ______________ crops all around this state.
6. We will move to a different ______________ next month.
7. Someday, we will stop moving. We will ______________ in a town.

MORE Key Words Practice

Make up a sentence using three of the Key Words.

Name ______________________ Date ____________

Vocabulary Skill

Figurative Language

Rewrite each sentence in your own words, without using *like*.

1. My family keeps moving, like a butterfly going from flower to flower.

   My family moves from place to place.

2. Our truck growls and roars like a lion.

   ____

3. The road curves and bends like a long snake.

   ____

What would it be like to sleep under the stars?

Rewrite each sentence in your own words. Use a comparison with *like*.

4. The ground feels hard.

   The ground is like cement.

5. The insects make noise.

   ____

   ____

6. The stars sparkle.

   ____

   ____

Name ______________________ Date ____________

Grammar: Present Perfect Tense

We Have Traveled

Write the present perfect tense of each verb to complete the sentence. Use the past participles in the box.

Present Perfect Tense

To form the **present perfect**, use the helping verb ***has*** or ***have*** plus the **past participle**. The past participle is one of the three **principal parts** of a verb.

Some Past Participles

worked	moved	enjoyed	spent
traveled	started	taught	brought

For many years, my father has worked (work) on farms in California. Our family ____________ (travel) with him. We ____________ (move) many times. We are glad that my father ____________ (bring) us with him. We ____________ (spend) some wonderful times together.

This season, I ____________ (start) to work with my father. The work is hard, but he ____________ (teach) me how to do it well. I ____________ (enjoy) working with him.

MORE Present Perfect Tense Verbs

Write a paragraph about something you have done. Choose something that started in the past and is still going on. Use present perfect tense verbs.

Name ______________________ Date ____________

Graphic Organizer: Character Chart

Calling the Doves

Review "Calling the Doves."

Study this example. Then use another sheet to complete two more rows for the chart. Make one row for Felipe and one for Juanito.

Character and Relationship to Juanito	Actions	Traits	Outcome and Reason
Lucha: mother	cooks good food creates a warm home wherever they are recites poetry	good cook and housekeeper kind loves her family loves poetry	She decides they must settle down so Juanito can go to school. She loves Juanito and wants to do what is best for him.

Name ______________________ Date ______________

Respond to Literature

Compare Two Characters

Compare Juanito in "Calling the Doves" with the boy in "Grandma's Records." Complete the Venn diagram.

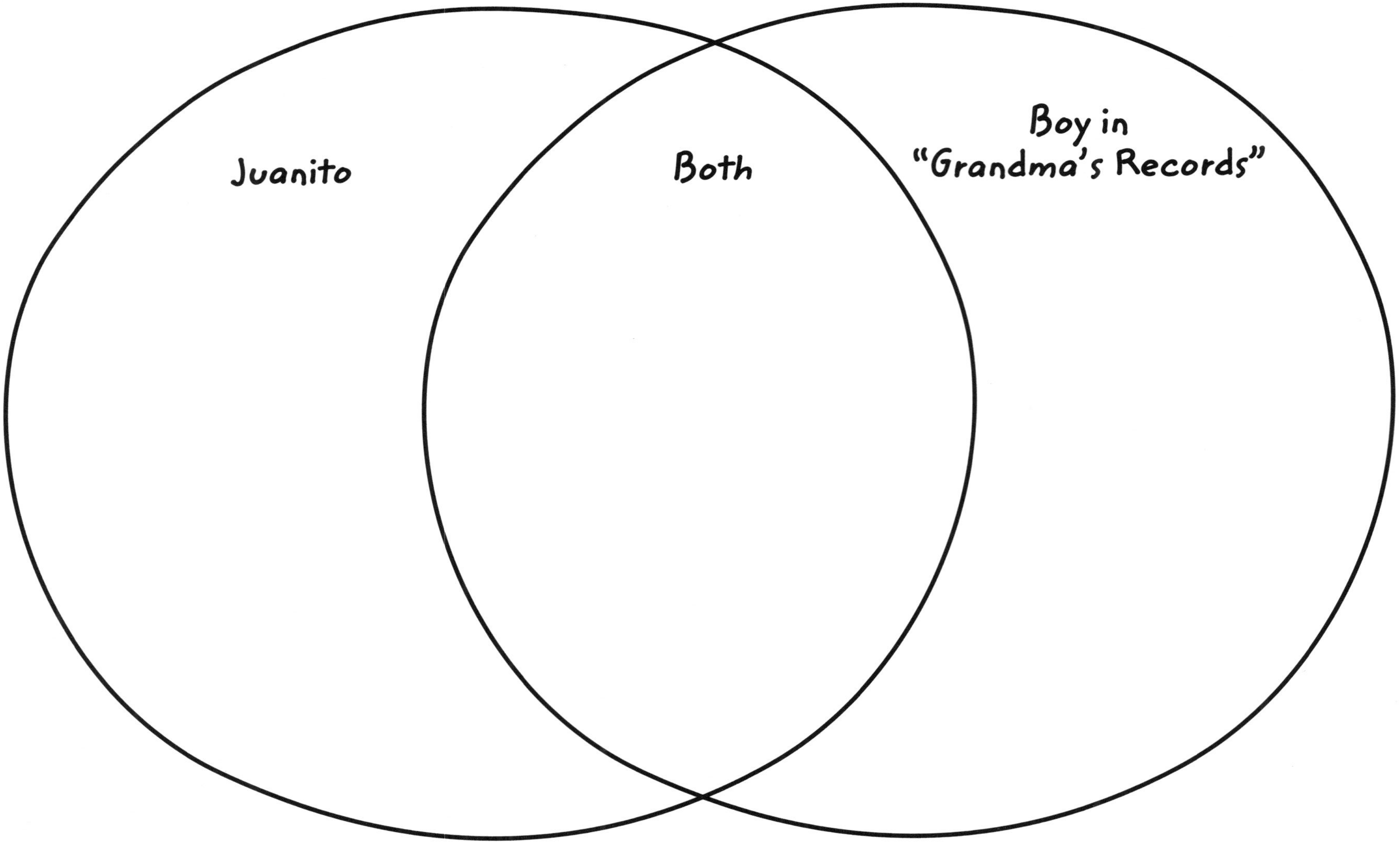

Name ______________________ Date __________

Comprehension Skill

Form Generalizations

Read the passage below. Think about how to form generalizations.

An International Building

1 My apartment building is international. That means people from many countries live here. One year people from eleven different countries lived here! My family came from Ecuador, a country in South America.

2 I have lots of friends in my building. My friend Danielle lives on the third floor. Her family is from France. They came to New York City two years ago.

3 Jimoh's family is from Nigeria. That is a country on the west coast of Africa. His father writes plays. We went to see one of his plays last summer.

4 Duarte lives next door. His family came here from Portugal before he was born. His father is a doctor. He works at a big hospital in our neighborhood.

5 Molly lives on the first floor. Her grandparents came here a long time ago. Molly's grandfather tells us funny stories about when he was a boy in Ireland. He lived near a real castle!

6 Every spring, we have a big party in our building. Everyone gets together and brings food. There is food from every country. Some people even dress up in traditional clothes and sing songs from their native lands. Last year, Duarte's mother sang a beautiful song in Portuguese. The spring party is a good way to meet new friends and try new food. Everyone has a great time!

Now take the test on page 136.

Name ______________________ Date ____________

Test Strategy
Look for key words like *best*. They will help you find the correct answer.

Read each item. Choose the best answer.

1 Which is the best generalization for paragraph 1 on page 136?

- ⬭ Many people in the building come from other countries.
- ⬭ People from other countries usually live in apartments.
- ⬭ Most apartment buildings are international.
- ⬭ Most people from Ecuador live in the building.

2 Which is the best generalization for paragraph 6 on page 136?

- ⬭ Most people like Portuguese songs.
- ⬭ People usually eat too much food.
- ⬭ Most people in New York love to go to a party.
- ⬭ Some people like to share food and songs with their neighbors from other countries.

3 Which generalization best fits the article?

- ⬭ Most people don't like people from other countries.
- ⬭ It's fun to live in a big building.
- ⬭ New York City is the best place to have parties.
- ⬭ People from different countries can be friends.

4 Which of the following is a generalization?

- ⬭ My friend Molly lives in the building.
- ⬭ Some people like to meet people from other countries.
- ⬭ My apartment building is in New York City.
- ⬭ Duarte's family came here before he was born.

Name ______________________ Date ______________

Literary Analysis

Character's Relationships and Changes

Think about stories you have read in which a character changes.

Complete the chart below for two characters from the same story or from different stories.

Character / Story	How the Character Changes	Who or What Causes the Change

Name ________________________ Date ____________

Vocabulary: Key Words

Words About Immigrants

Key Words
culture
descendant
distant relative
explorer
immigrant
pioneer
settler

Write a Key Word to complete each sentence.

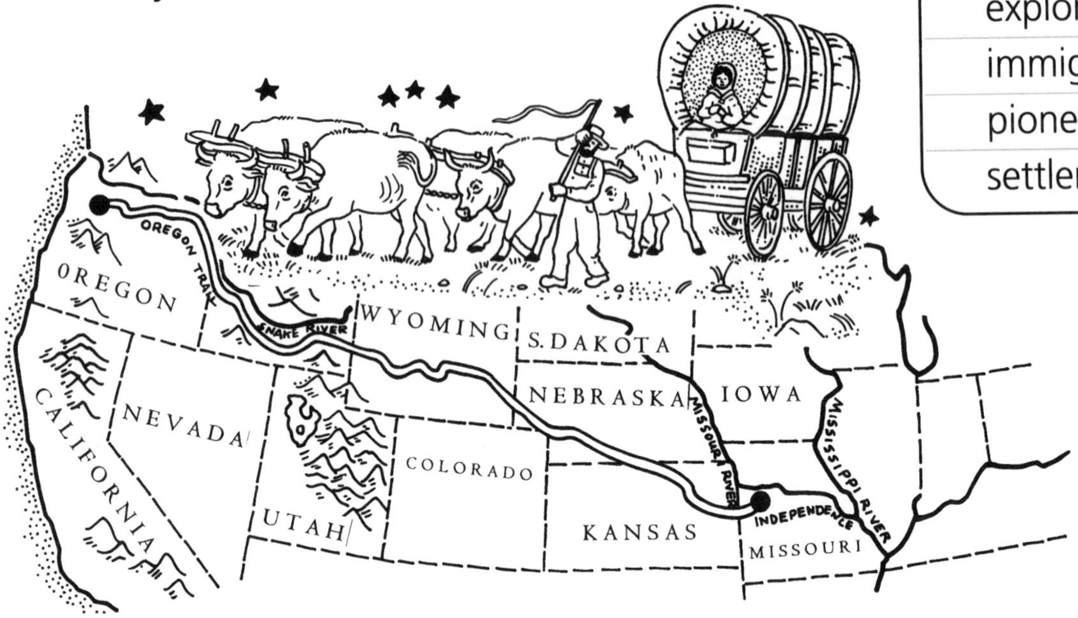

I am a ______________ (1.) of my grandmother Carla. She came here from another country. She was an ______________ (2.).

We have a ______________ (3.) who came to America long ago. He was an ______________ (4.) who went to different places to learn about them. After he came to America, he became a ______________ (5.), and he moved west in a covered wagon. His brother moved west, too. He was a ______________ (6.) in Texas. They moved to a new land, but they never forgot the ______________ (7.) of their home country.

Name ______________________ Date __________

Grammar: Present Perfect Tense

Fifteen Questions Game

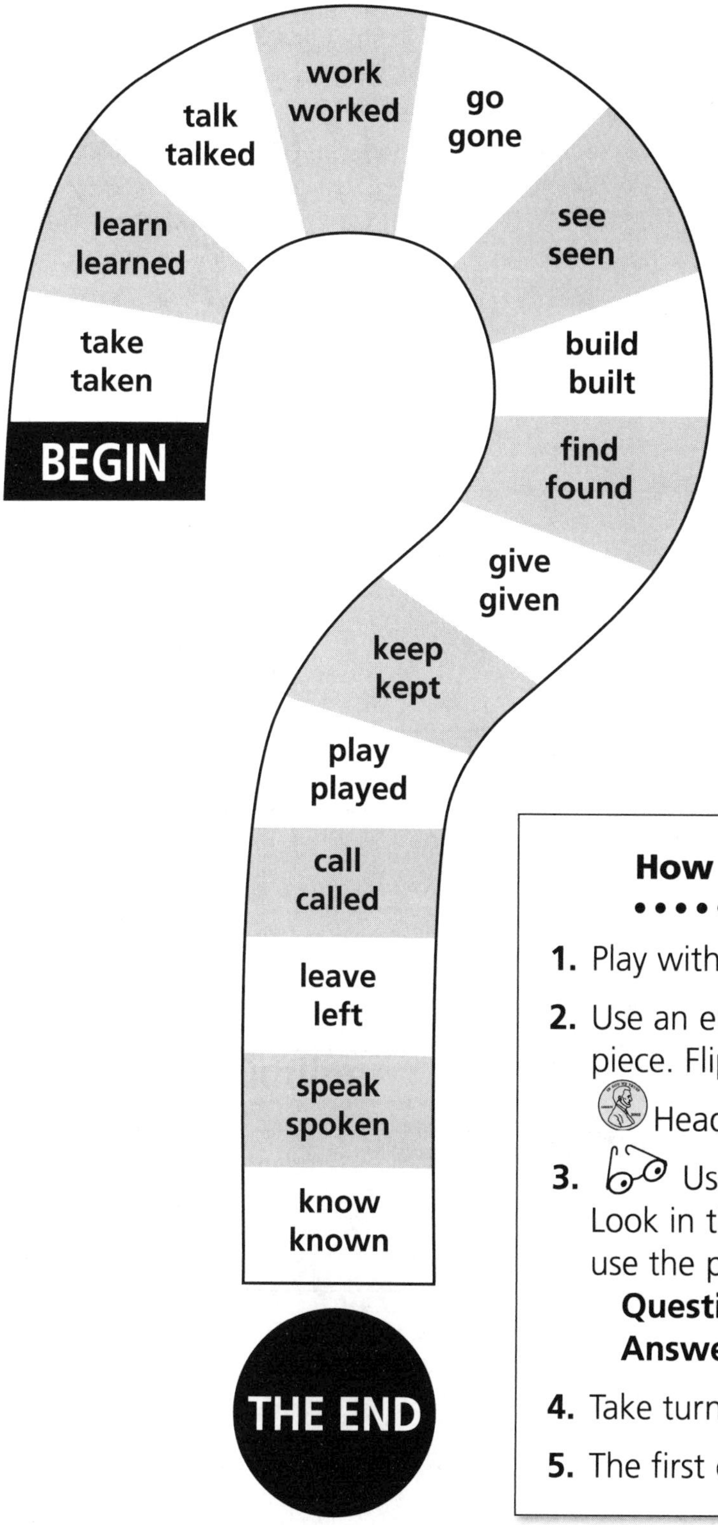

How to Play Fifteen Questions

1. Play with a partner.
2. Use an eraser or other small object as a game piece. Flip a coin to move.
   Heads = 1 space   Tails = 2 spaces
3. Use the past participle to ask a question. Look in the story for ideas. Have your partner use the past participle to answer. For example:
   Question: *Have you seen the doves?*
   Answer: *Yes, I have seen the doves.*
4. Take turns asking and answering questions.
5. The first one to reach **THE END** wins.

Name ______________________ Date ____________

Grammar: Past Perfect Tense

Looking into the Past

When did you learn to do different things as you were growing up?

Ask your family for information.

Write a sentence telling about something you had already done at each age. Use *had* plus the past participle of a verb.

I had learned to ride a bike before I was six years old.

Your Age		
2	**1.**	______________________
4	**2.**	______________________
6	**3.**	______________________
8	**4.**	______________________
9	**5.**	______________________
10	**6.**	______________________

Name ______________________ Date ____________

Grammar: Past Perfect Tense

This Had Happened Before

Look through "Coming to America" again. Find two events that happened at different times.

Write a sentence that tells about both events. Use a past perfect verb.

Past Perfect Tense

To form the **past perfect**, use the helping verb ***had*** plus the **past participle**.

had built

When you tell about two events in a sentence, use the past perfect with the event that happened first.

The Incas **had built** great cities before the Europeans arrived in America.

1. Many Africans had come to America by the time workers completed the transcontinental railroad.
2. ______________________
3. ______________________
4. ______________________
5. ______________________

MORE Past Perfect Tense

In one sentence, tell a partner about two events in your life.

Remember to use *had* plus the past participle for the event that happened first.

Name ______________________ Date ____________

Graphic Organizer: Classification Chart

Coming to America

Review "Coming to America." Complete the chart.

Time Period	Who Came	Why They Came
thousands of years ago	Native Americans	to hunt and settle in the new land
1000–1600s	European explorers, European settlers	
1600s	African slaves	
1700s	more Europeans	
mid-1800s		
1820–1925		
1925–today		

Name ____ Date ________________

Research Skill

Table of Contents

Use the information on the pages to complete the Table of Contents below.

Make a Table of Contents

- List the titles of the chapters in the order in which they appear.
- Write the page number next to the title.

Building the Railroads	Americans Push West	Over the Rockies	On to the Pacific!	The Ohio Valley
32	6	24	42	16

Table of Contents

Chapter	Page
______________________________	______
______________________________	______
______________________________	______
______________________________	______
______________________________	______

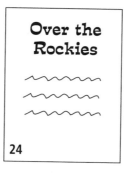

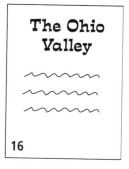

Name ______________________ Date ____________

Grammar: Helping Verbs

We Have Enjoyed It!

Write the present perfect tense of each verb to complete the sentence.

My relatives ______________ (live) in West Virginia for 75 years. Our whole family ______________ (settle) in this area.

My parents ______________ (open) a restaurant in our town. Many people ______________ (say) that my parents serve the best food in the state!

My sister ______________ (decide) to become a doctor. She ______________ (begin) to study at a nearby college.

My family ______________ (do) very well in this town. We ______________ (tell) our relatives in Lebanon to think about moving here, too. They ______________ (visit) us here. They ______________ (enjoy) their visits very much. I hope that they come back to stay.

MORE Helping Verbs

Ask your relatives about your family history.

Write a paragraph about where your family has lived and what they have done. Use the present perfect tense.